I0504687

AI VOODOO COLORING BOOK

Hey there, I'm Jeremy Hubert Burt. I was feeling inspired and decided to use a prompt to create some 3D coloring book pages. The prompt I used was:

"Design a captivating coloring book page featuring a mesmerizing Voodoo symbol. Against a pristine white background, use bold black lines to illustrate the intricate details of the symbol, creating an aura of mystery and fascination.

Create ornate and intricate background designs that complement the Voodoo symbol, adding an element of enchantment and allure. These designs should evoke a sense of wonder and curiosity.

Incorporate various shapes like swirling patterns, intricate curves, and symbolic elements throughout the page, immersing the viewer in the mystical world of Voodoo. Add captivating phrases in a font that captures the essence of magic and mysticism, enhancing the sense of intrigue and discovery.

Outline the symbol with bold black lines, clearly defining the boundaries for coloring. This empowers enthusiasts to infuse the symbol with their own creative energy and interpretation, using the striking contrast of black and white.

The coloring book page promises a captivating journey into the realm of Voodoo symbolism. It invites individuals to explore and engage in the art of coloring, providing a delightful sense of relaxation and stress relief. Embrace the enigmatic power of the Voodoo symbol amidst the timeless contrast of black and white."

After creating the design, I decided to edit the levels in GIMP in greyscale image mode to give it that extra touch of depth and detail. The whole process only took me a day, and I'm really happy with the results. I even published the pages using the Sqribble ebook maker, which was super easy to use. Check out the link if you want to Publish Your eBook: https://bit.ly/3nVzjvK.

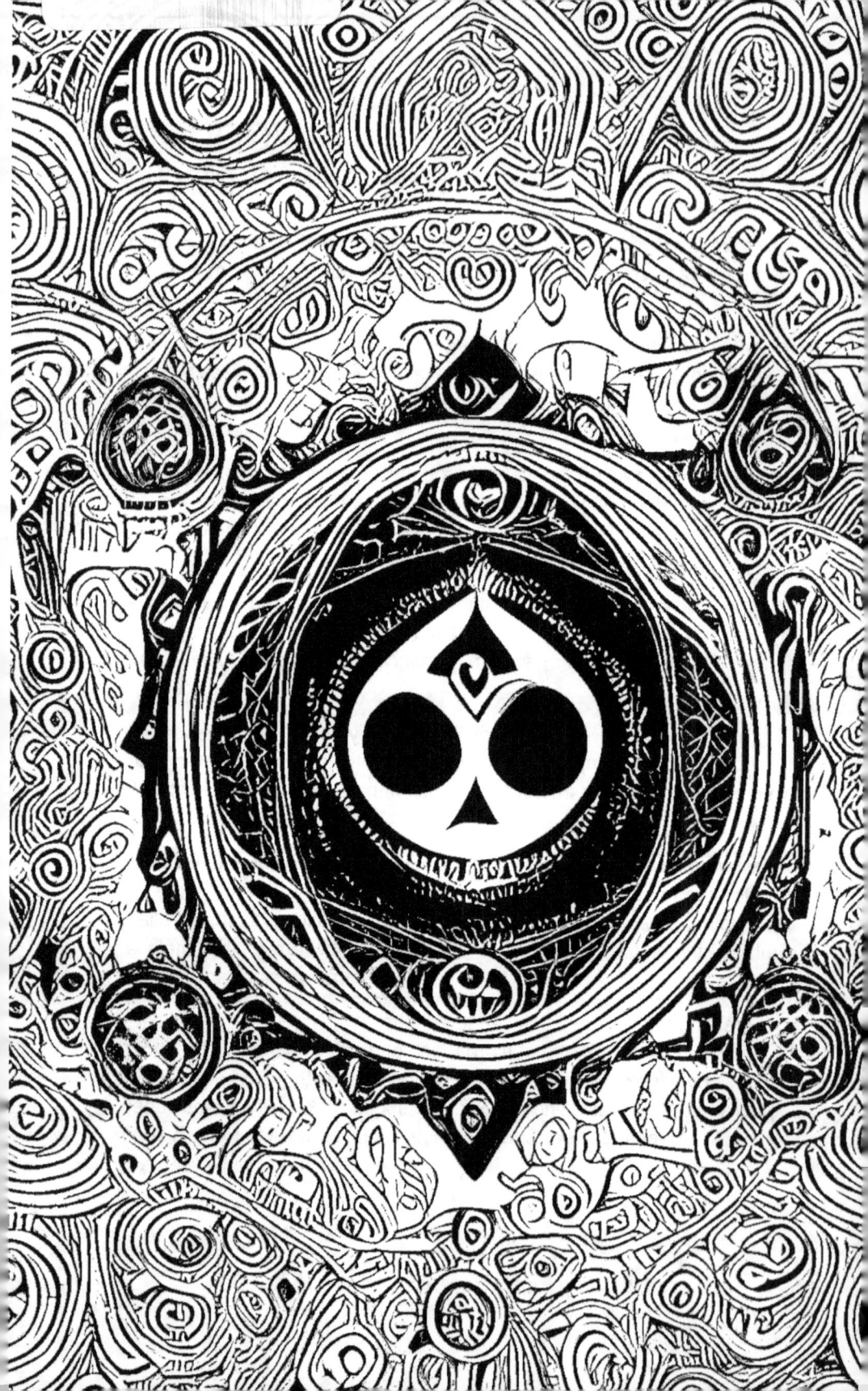

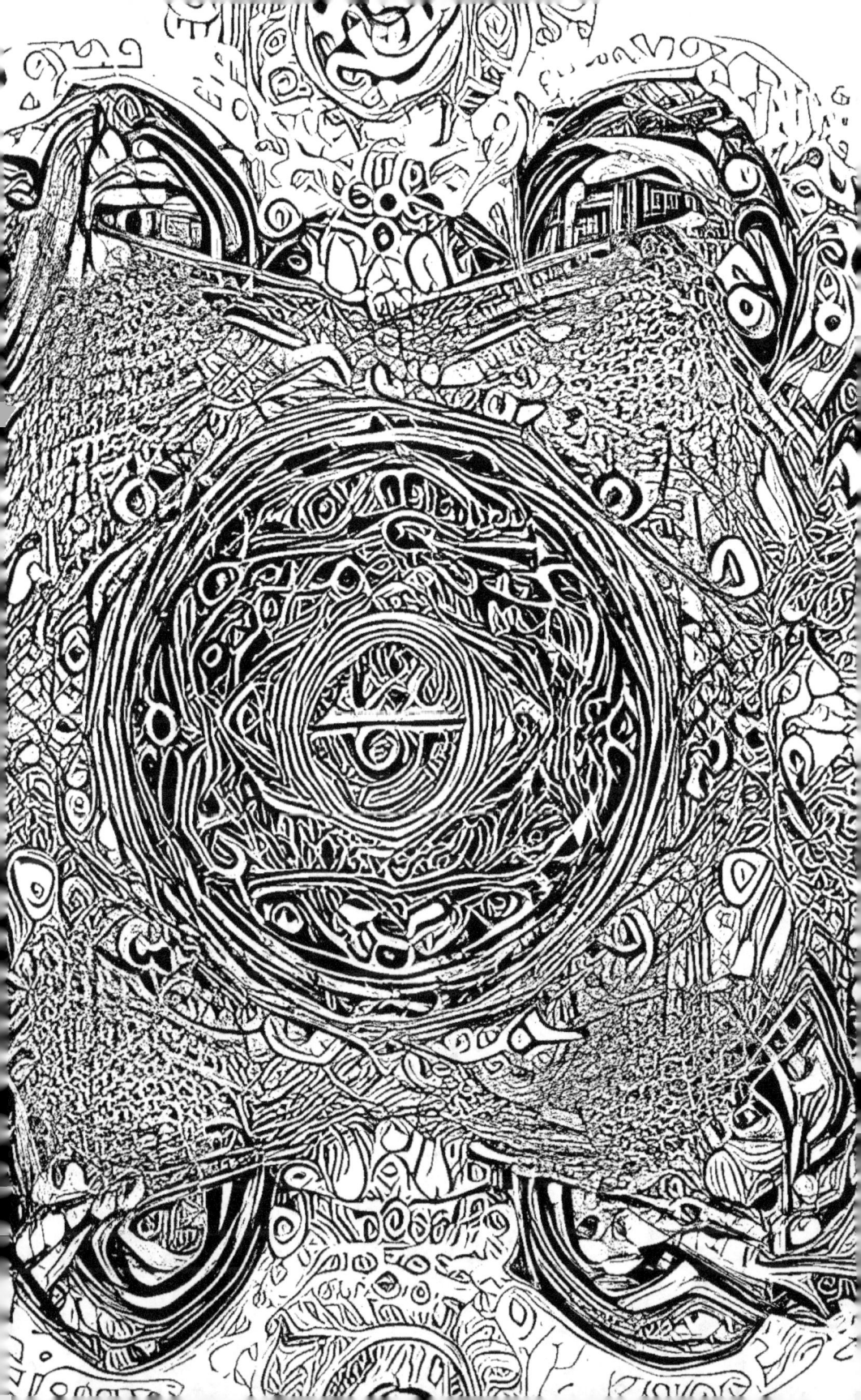

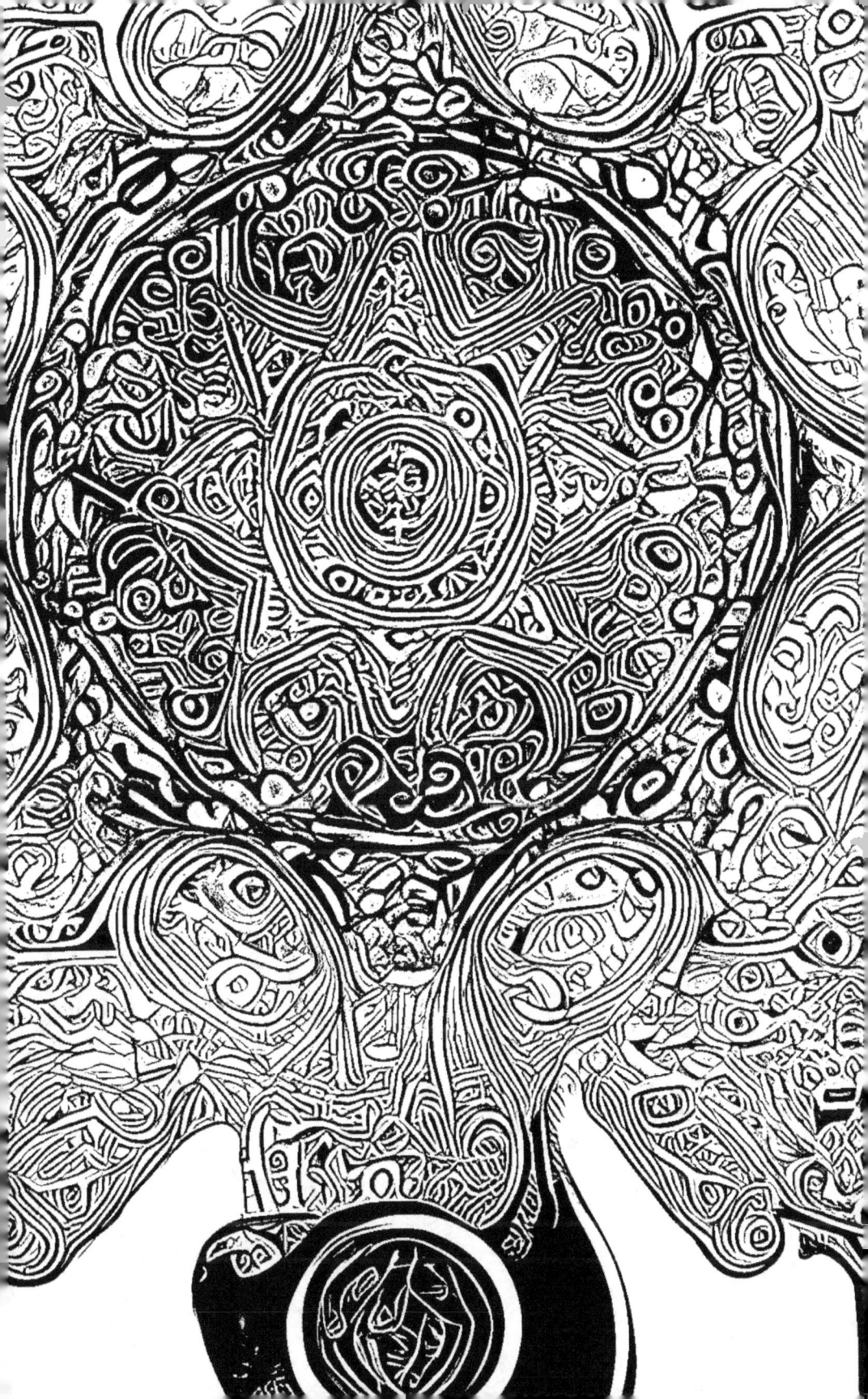

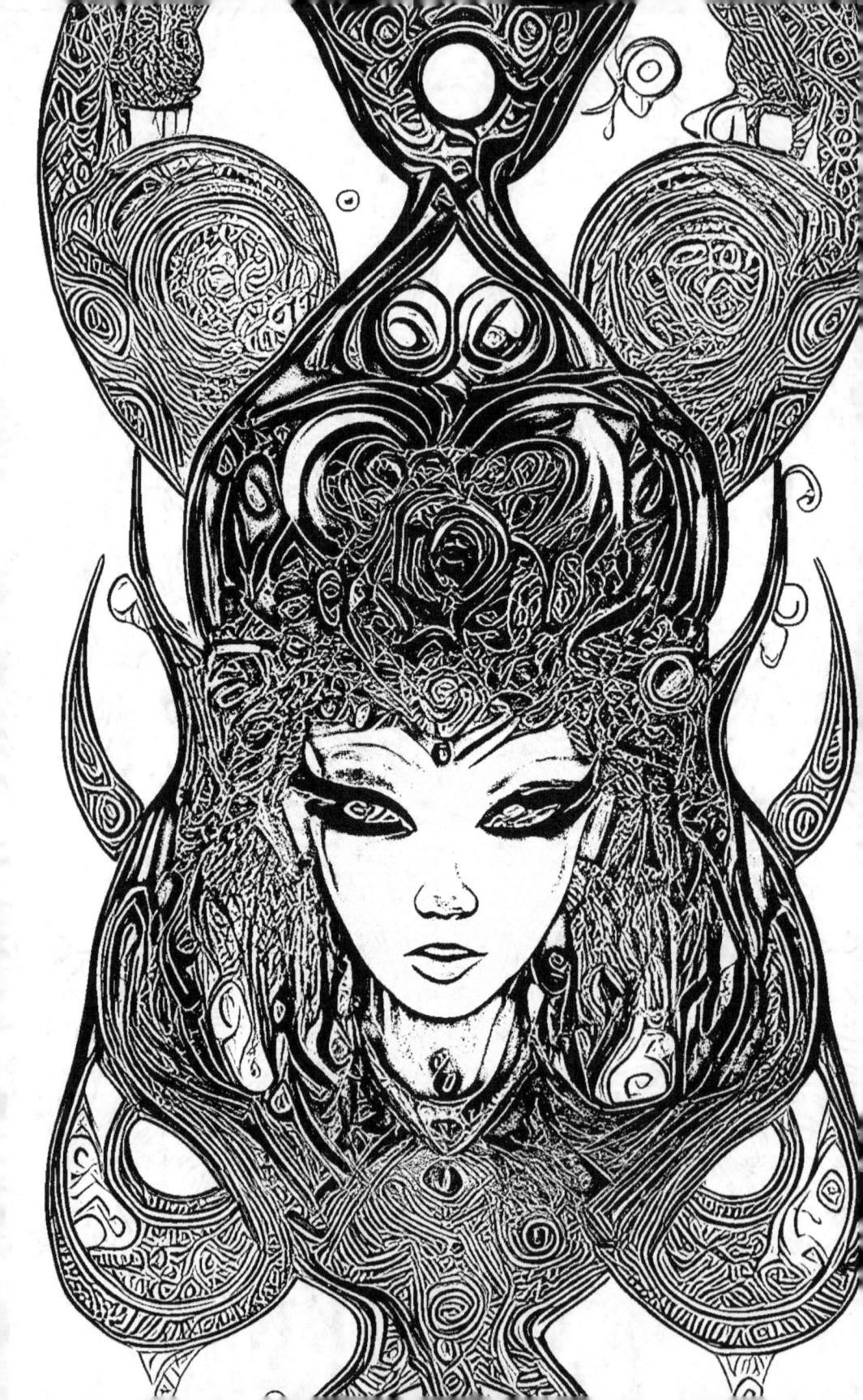

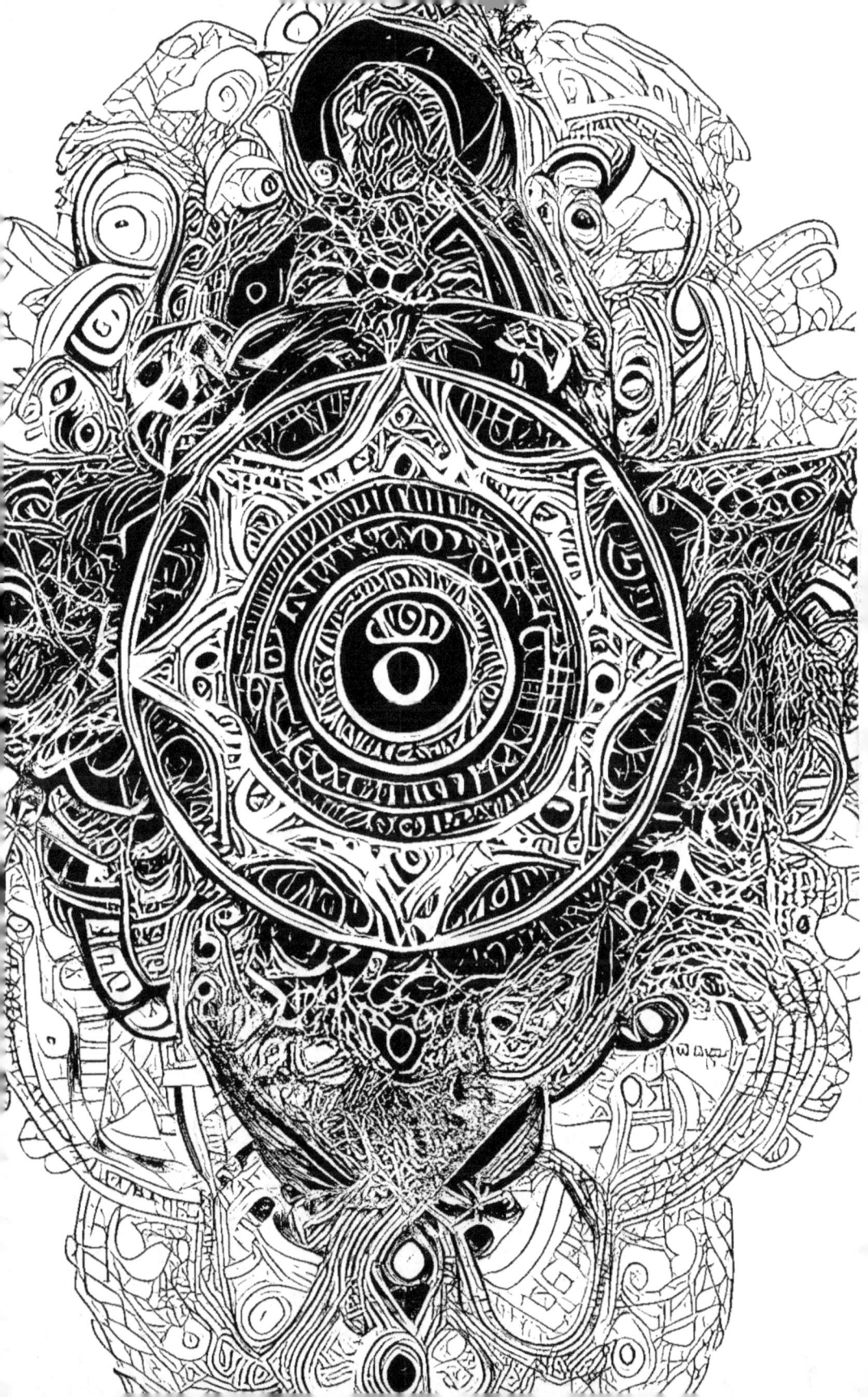

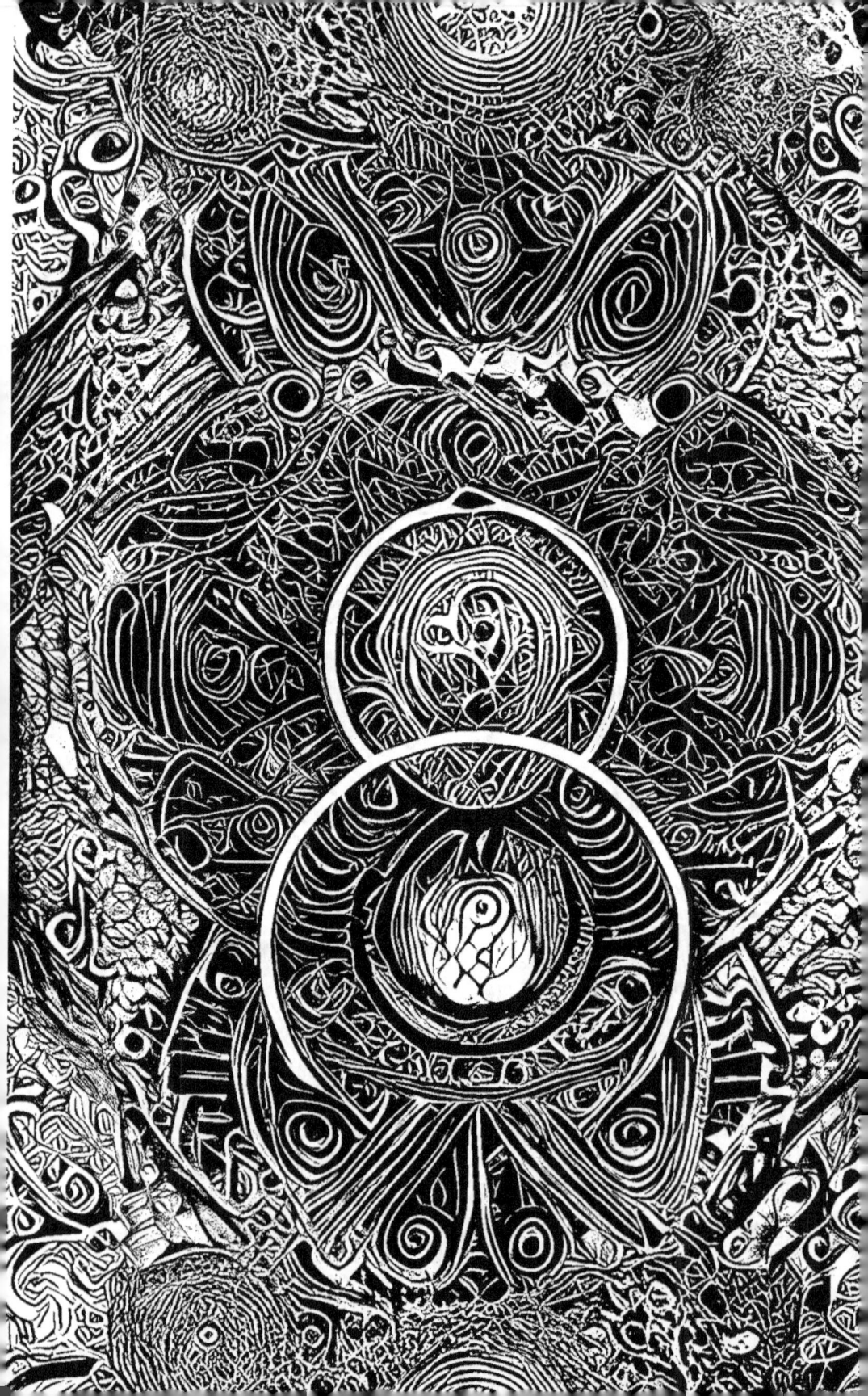

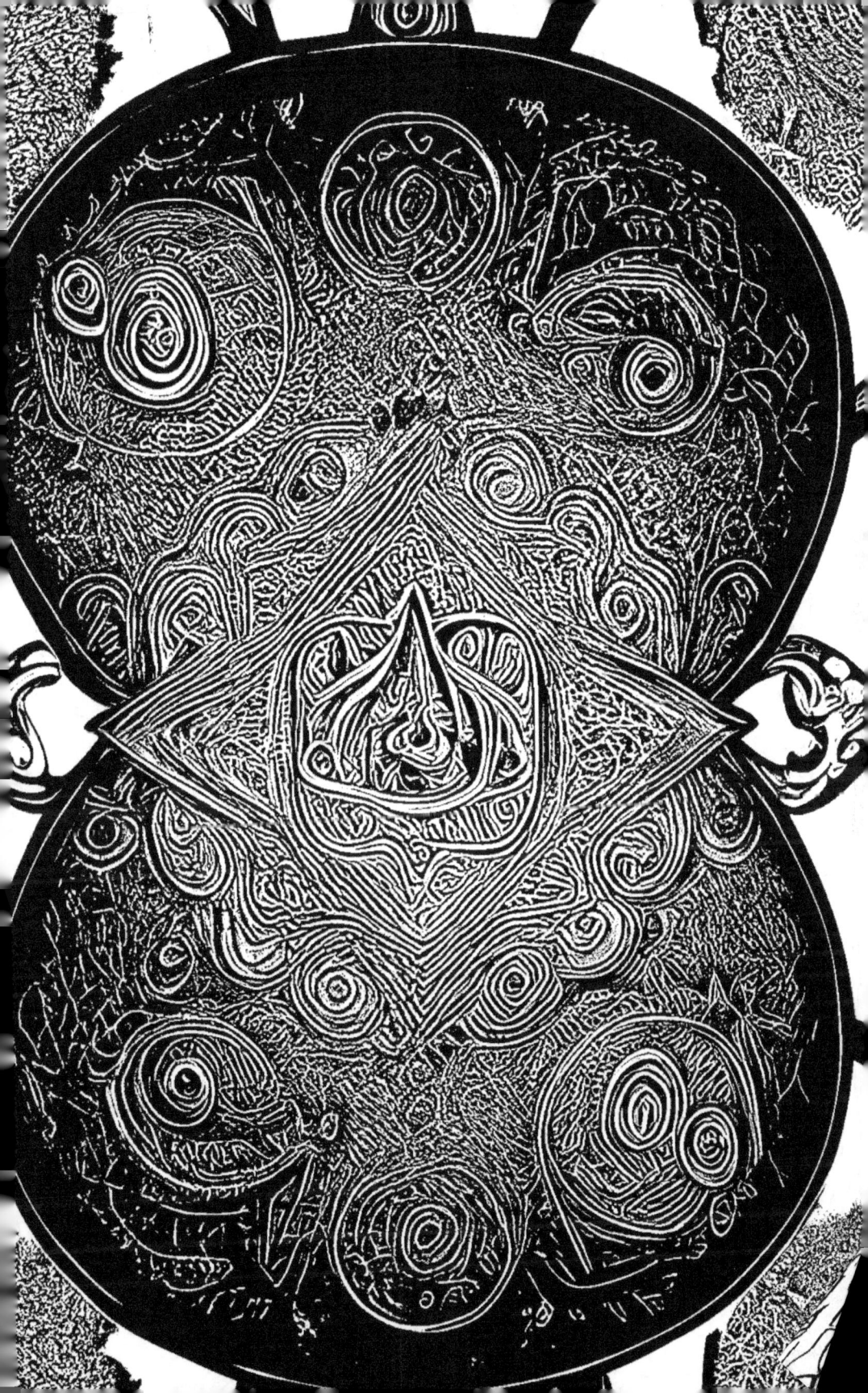

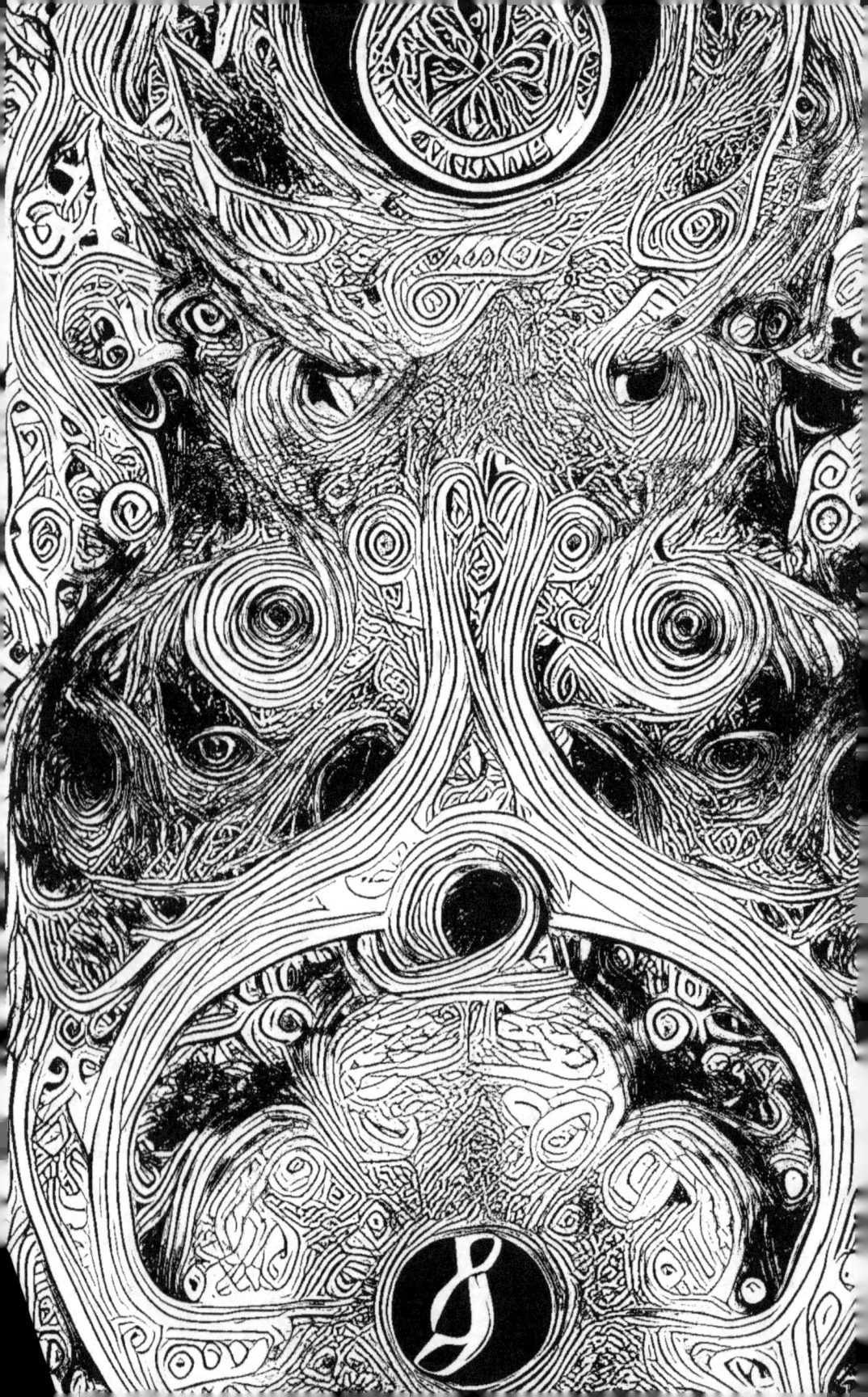

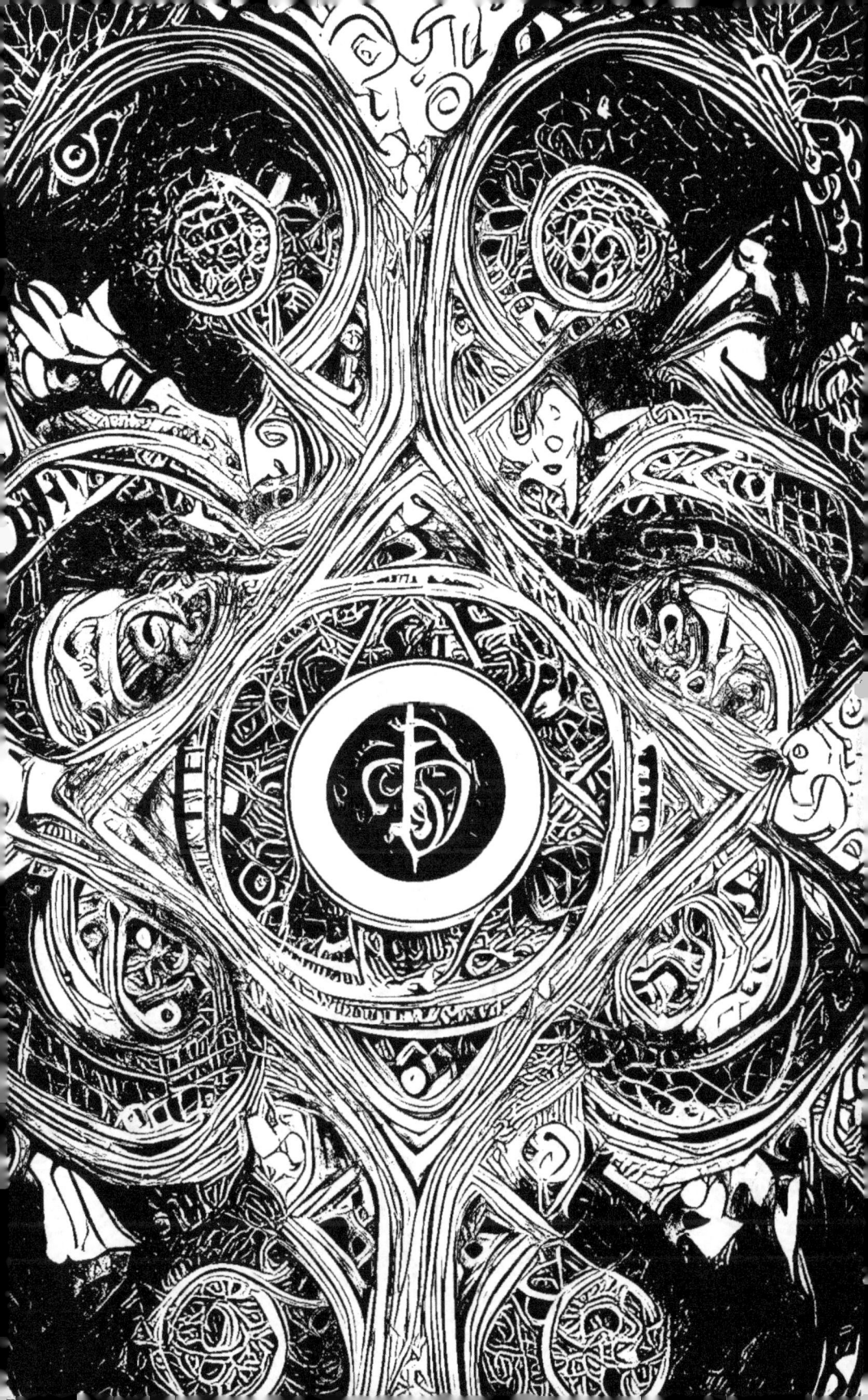

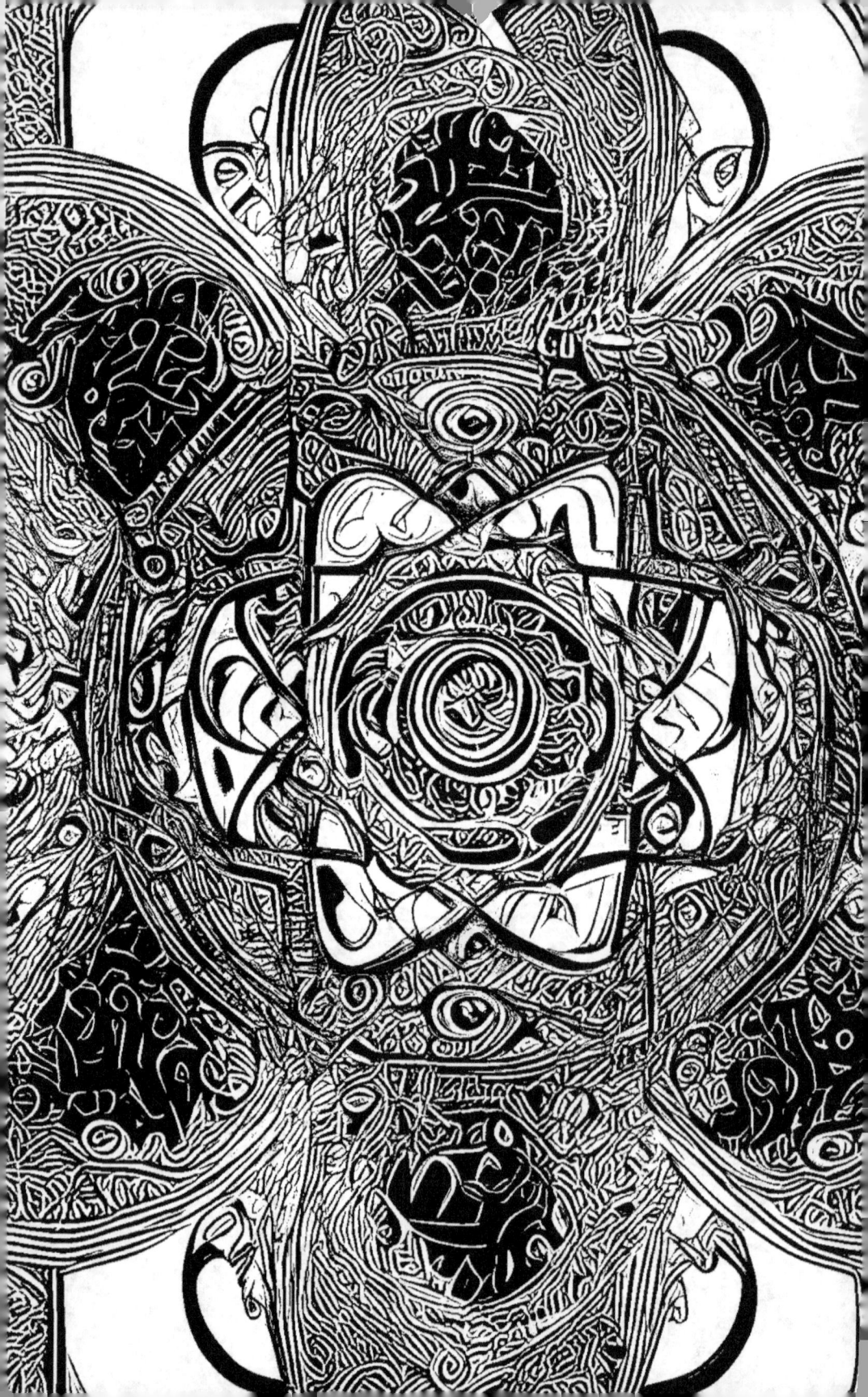

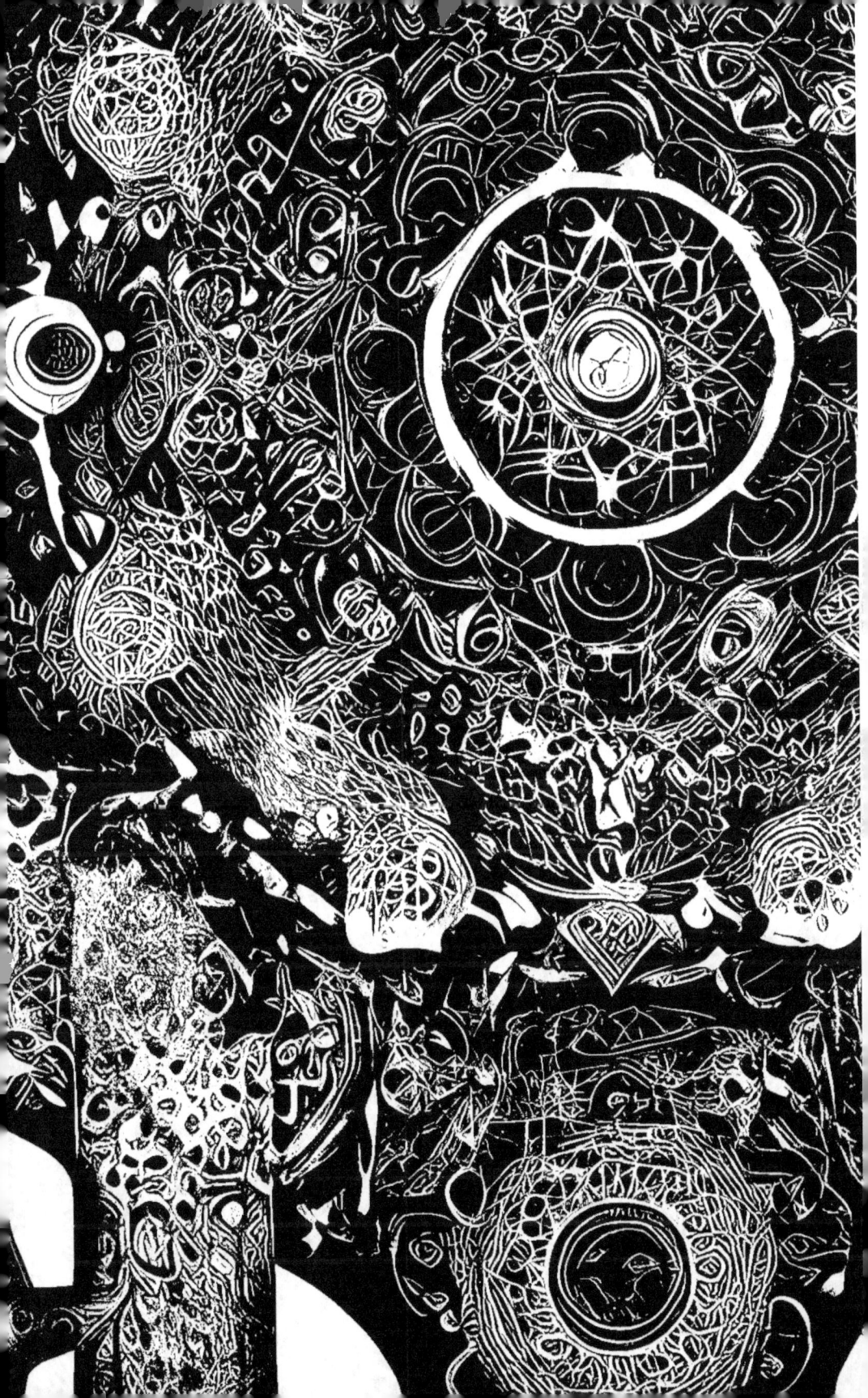

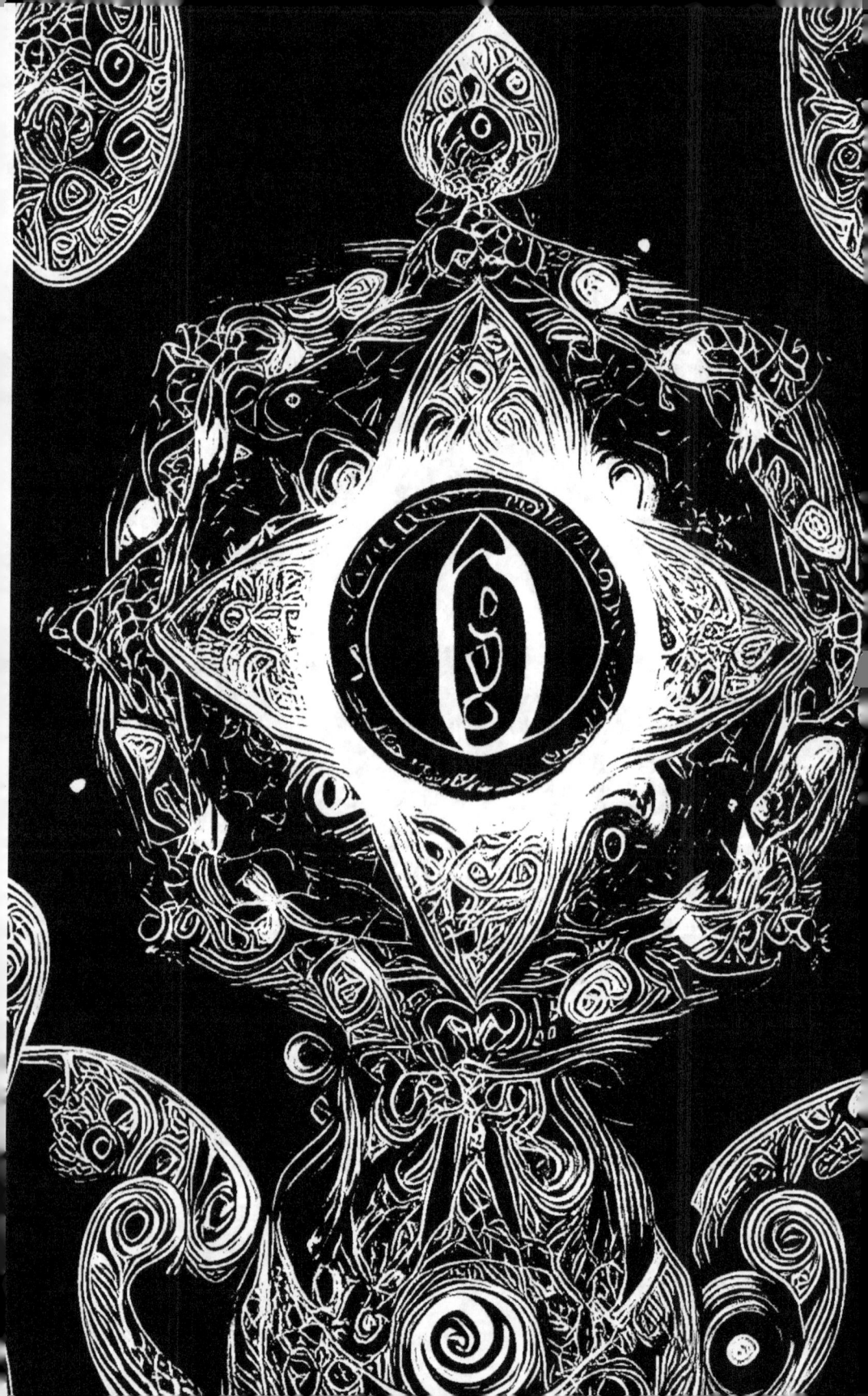

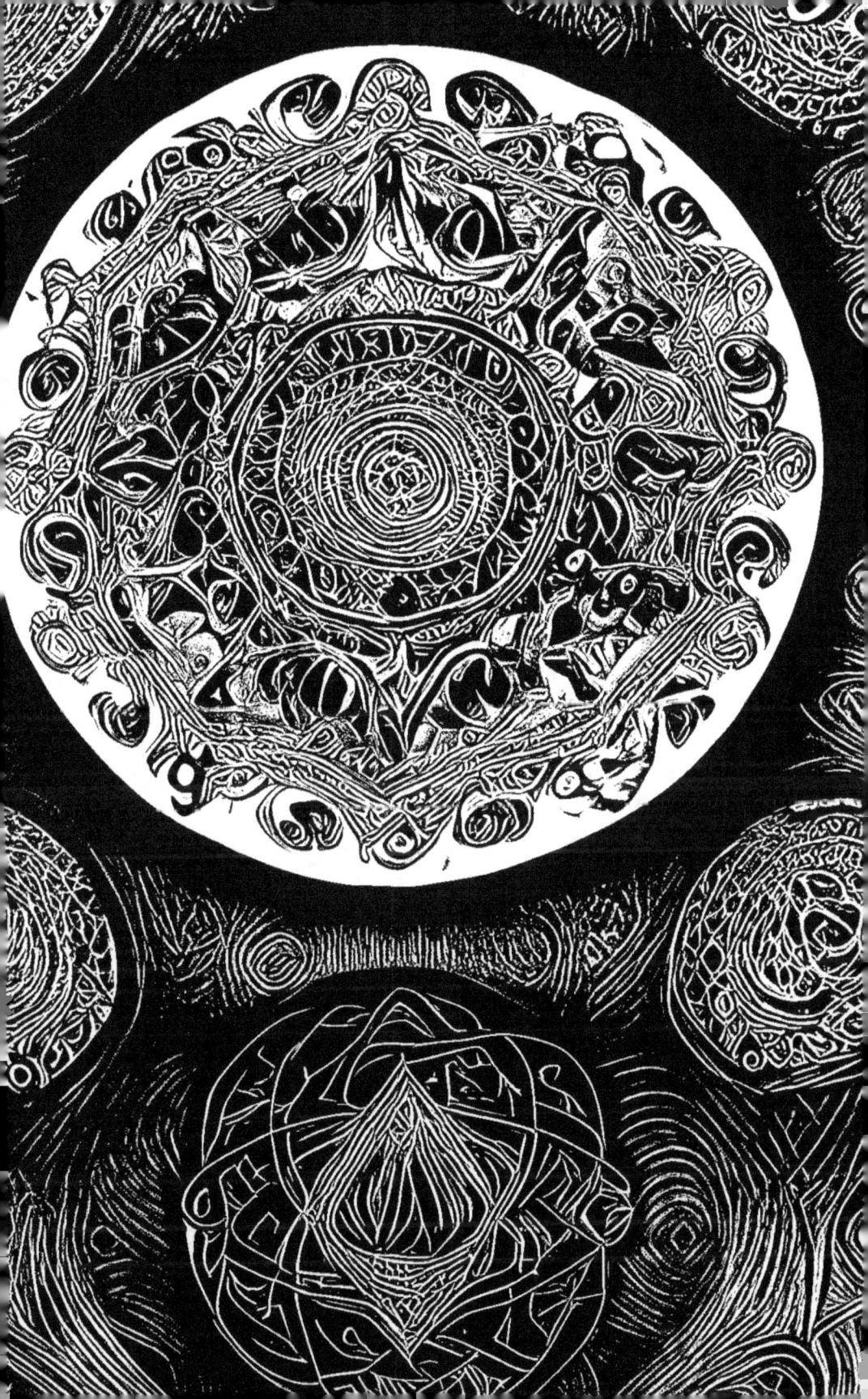

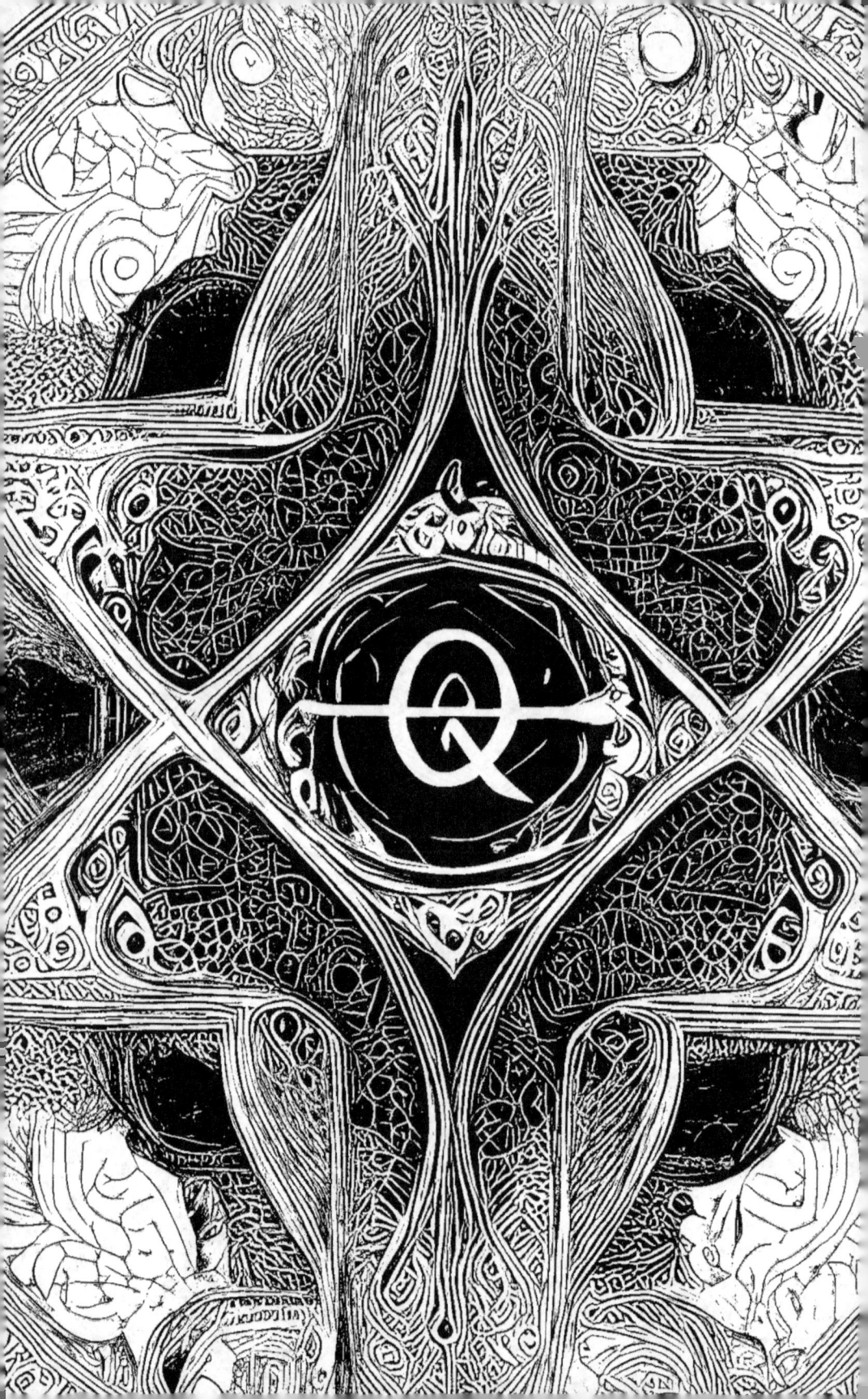

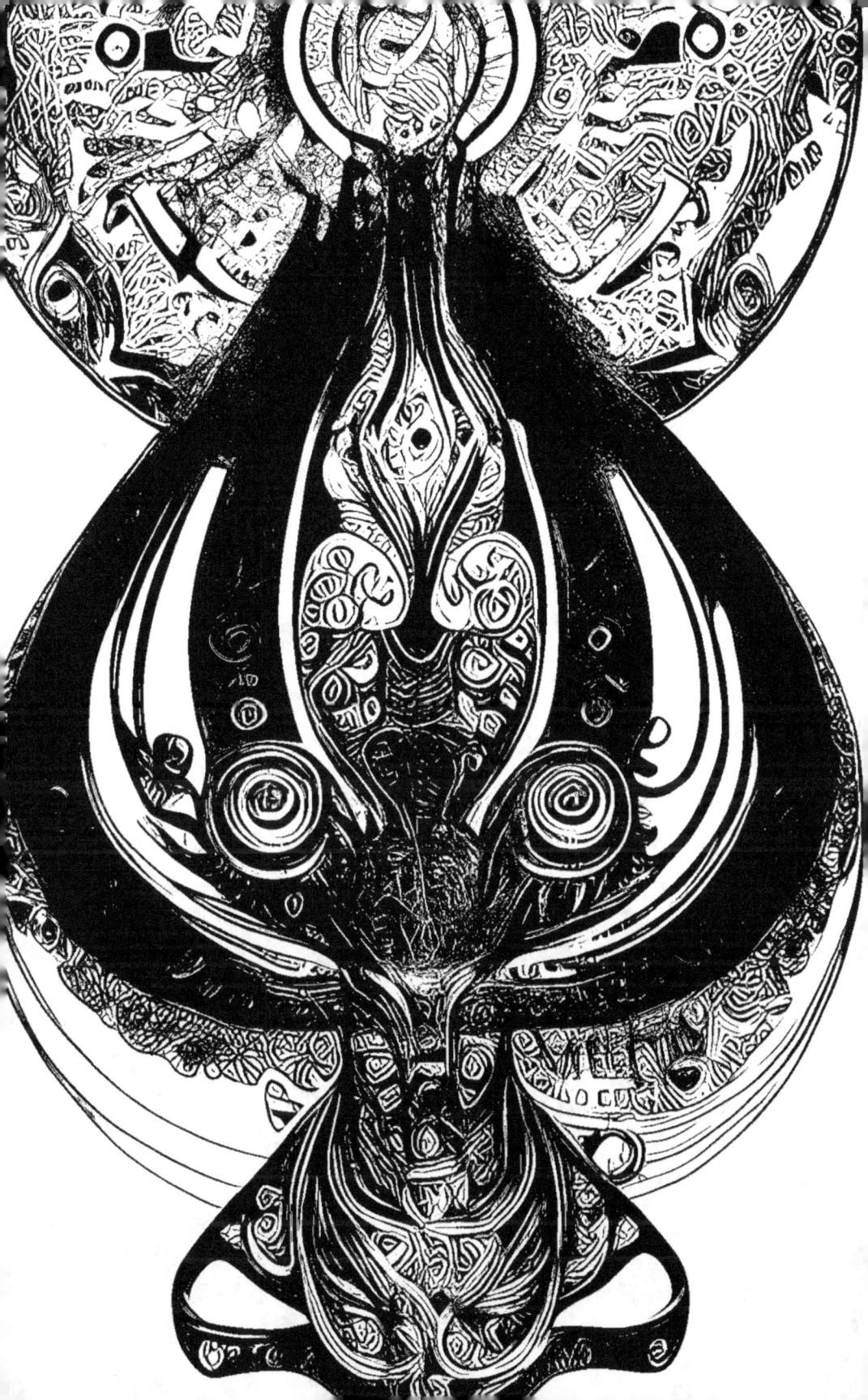

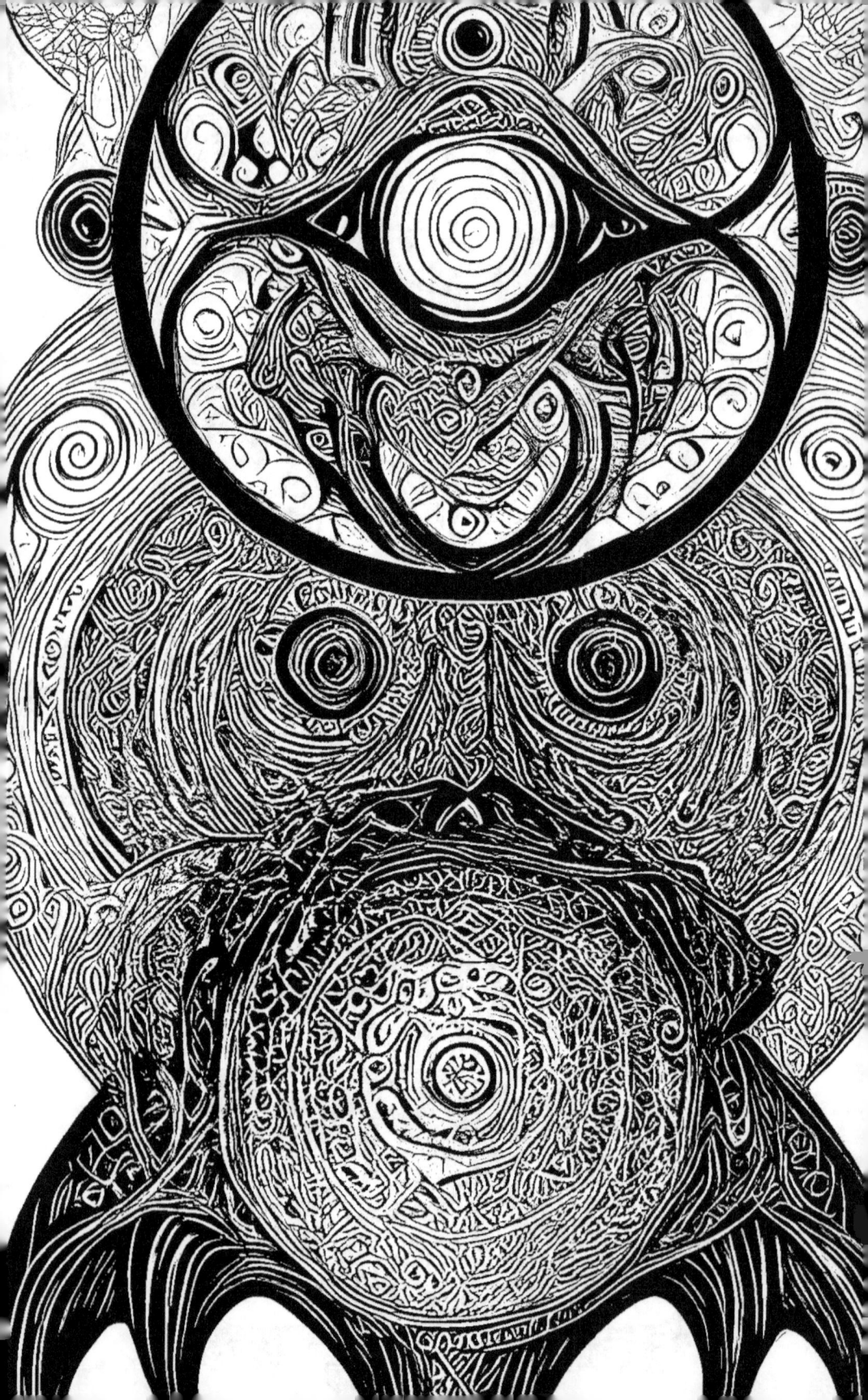

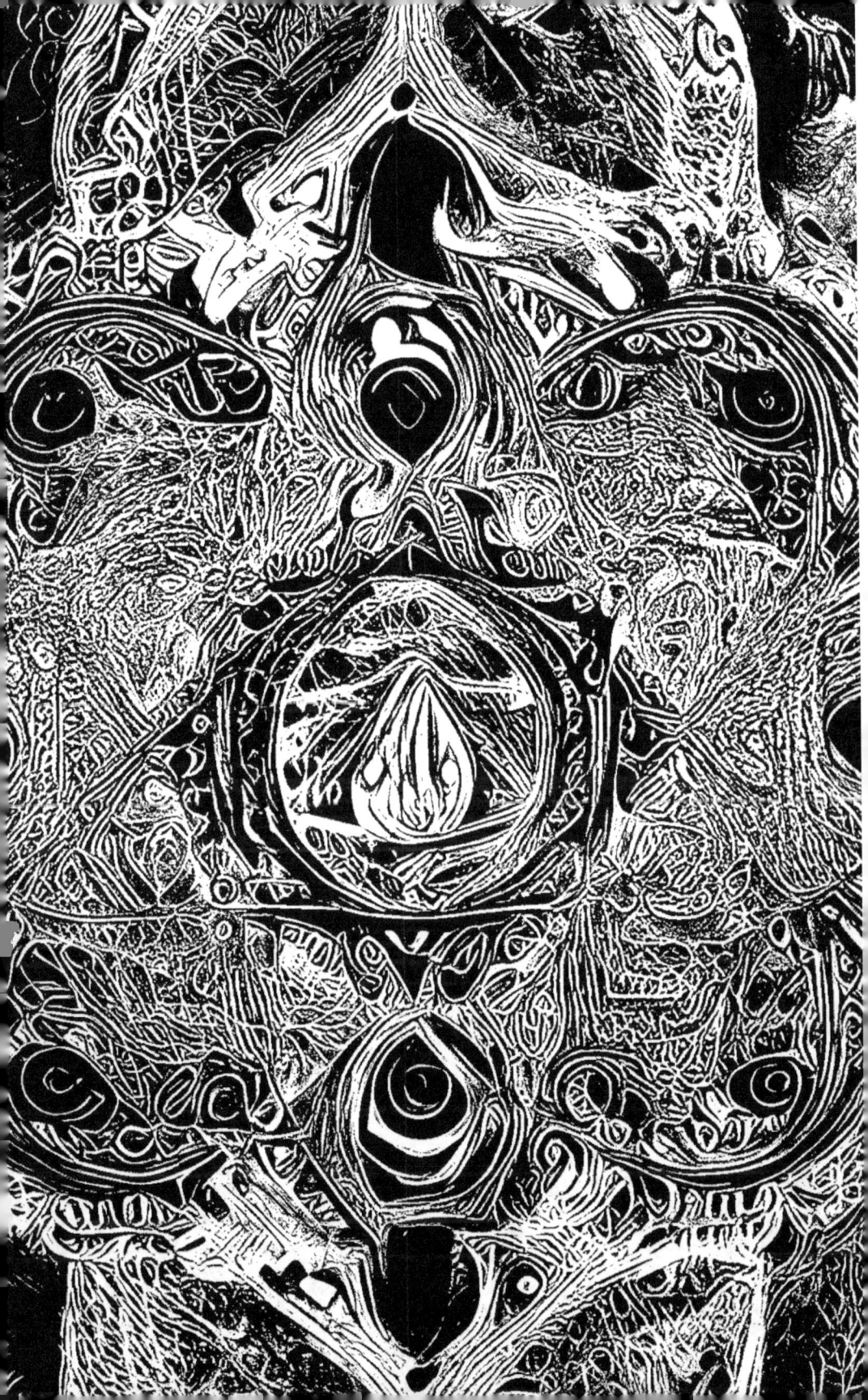

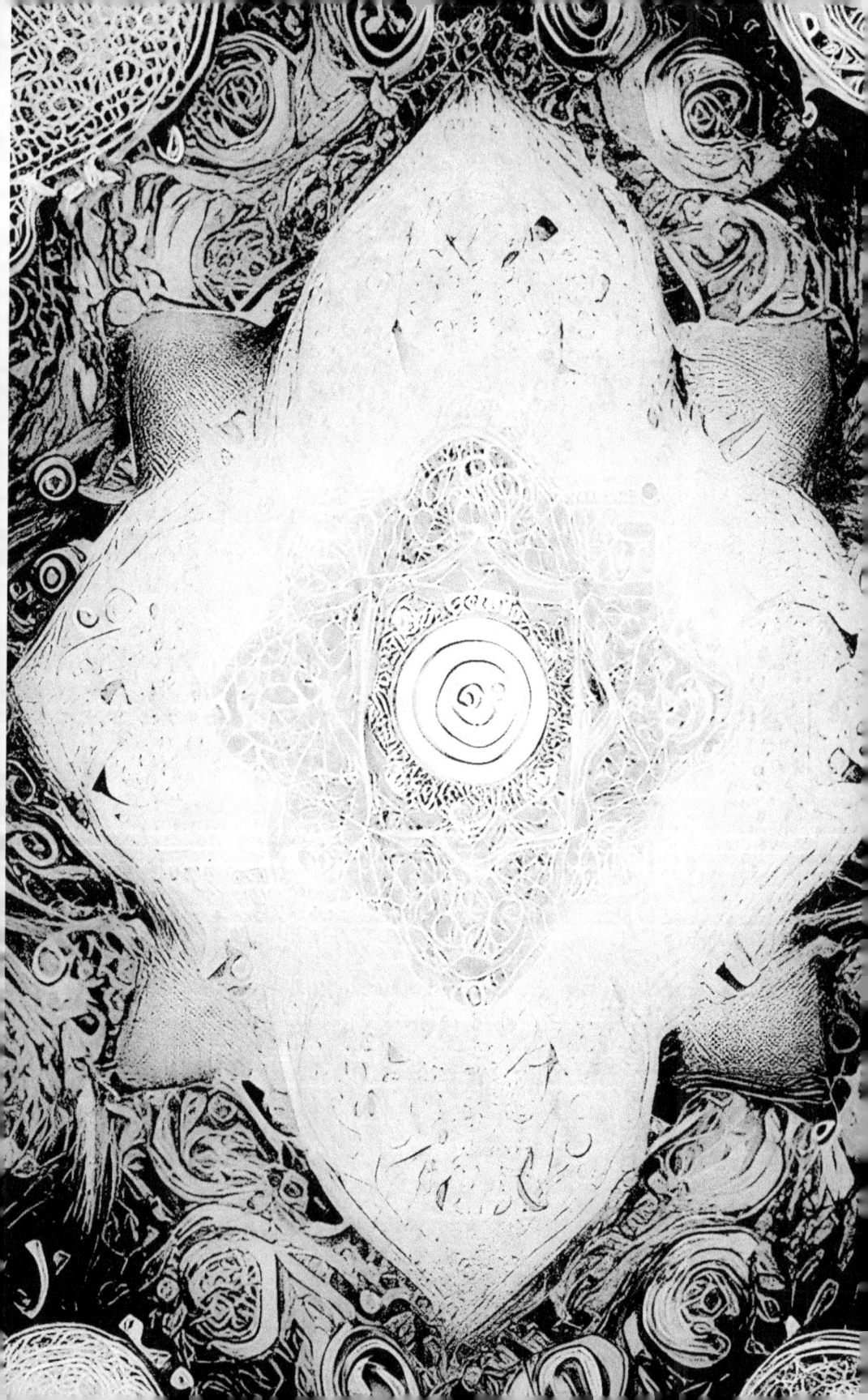

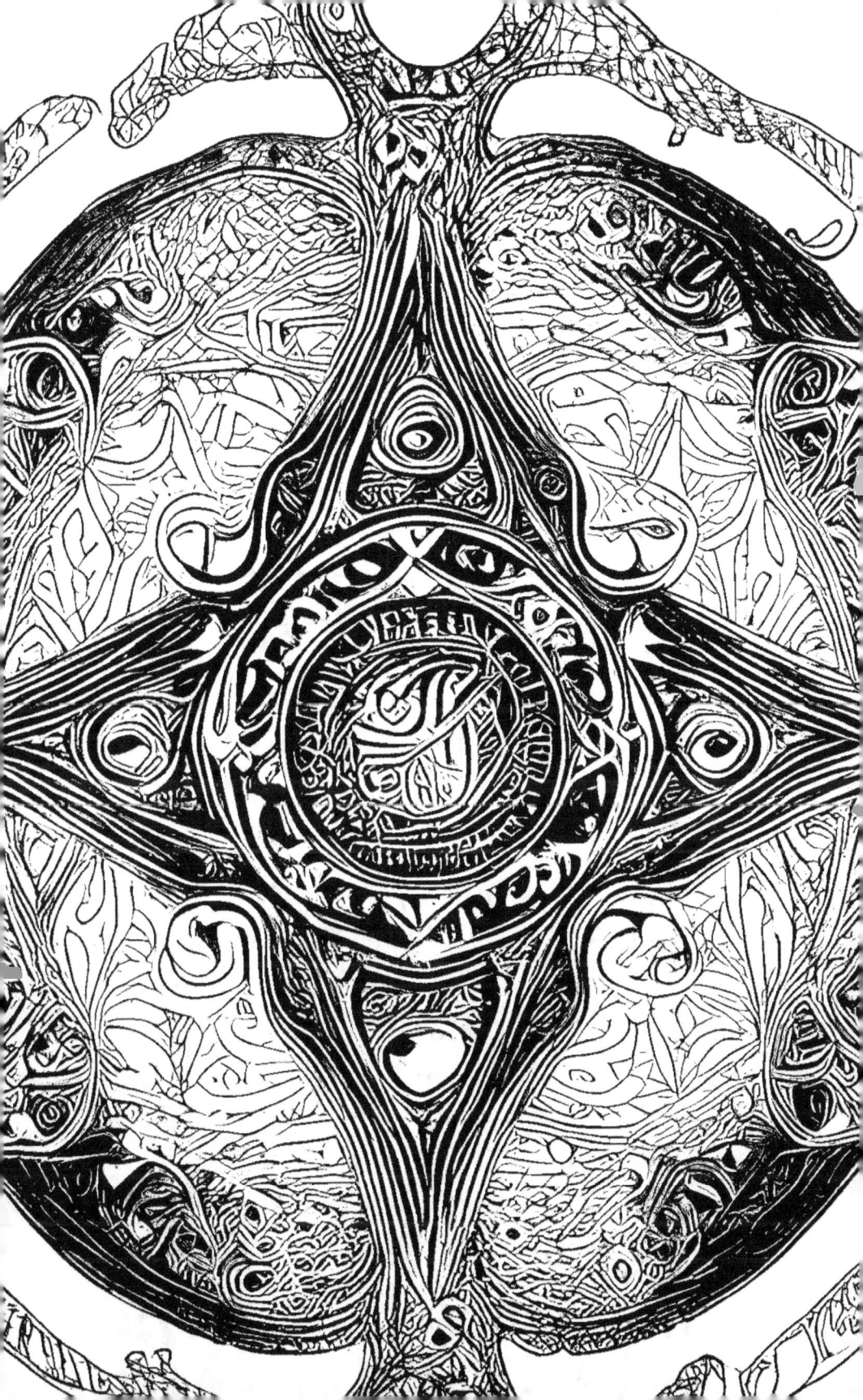

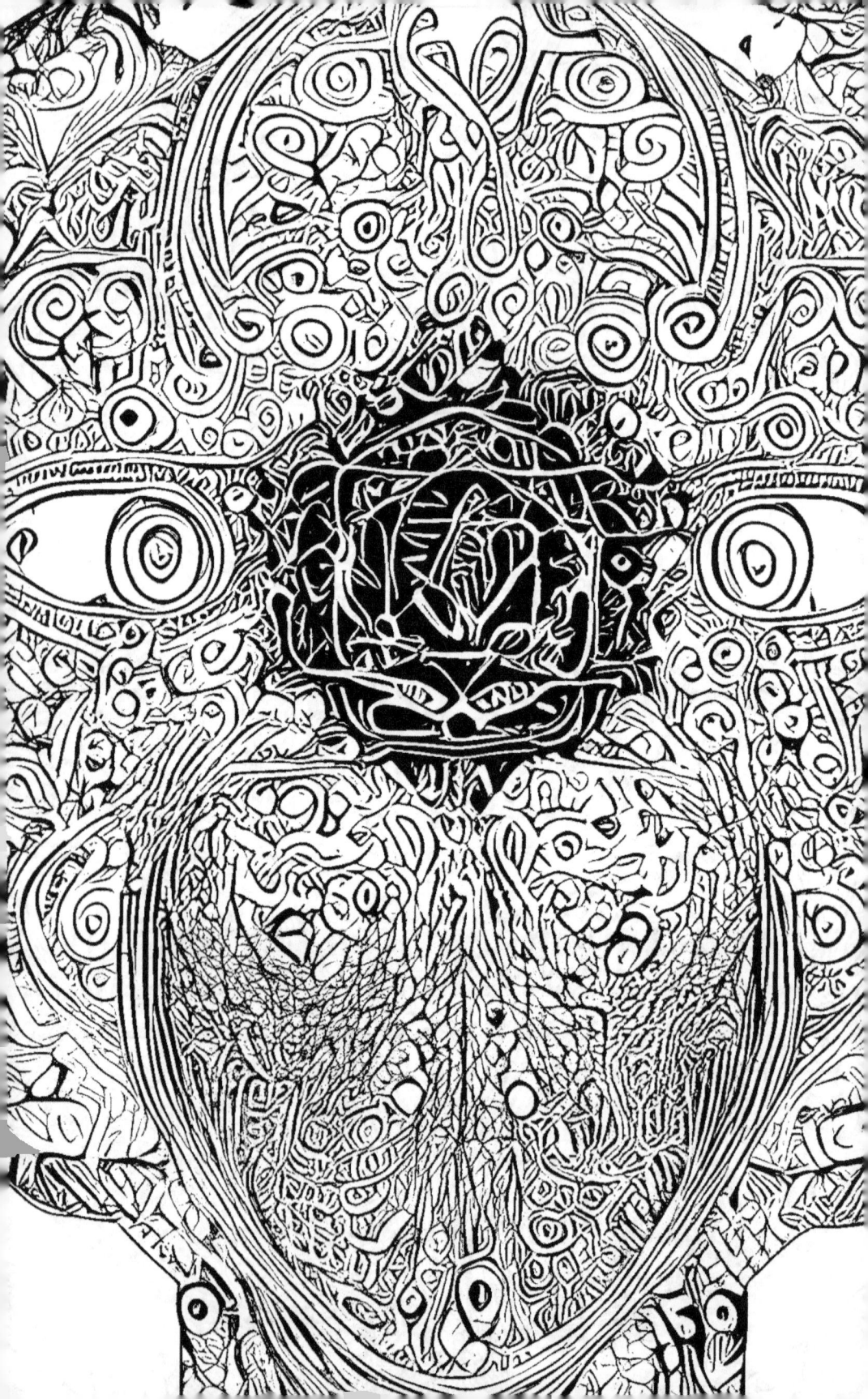

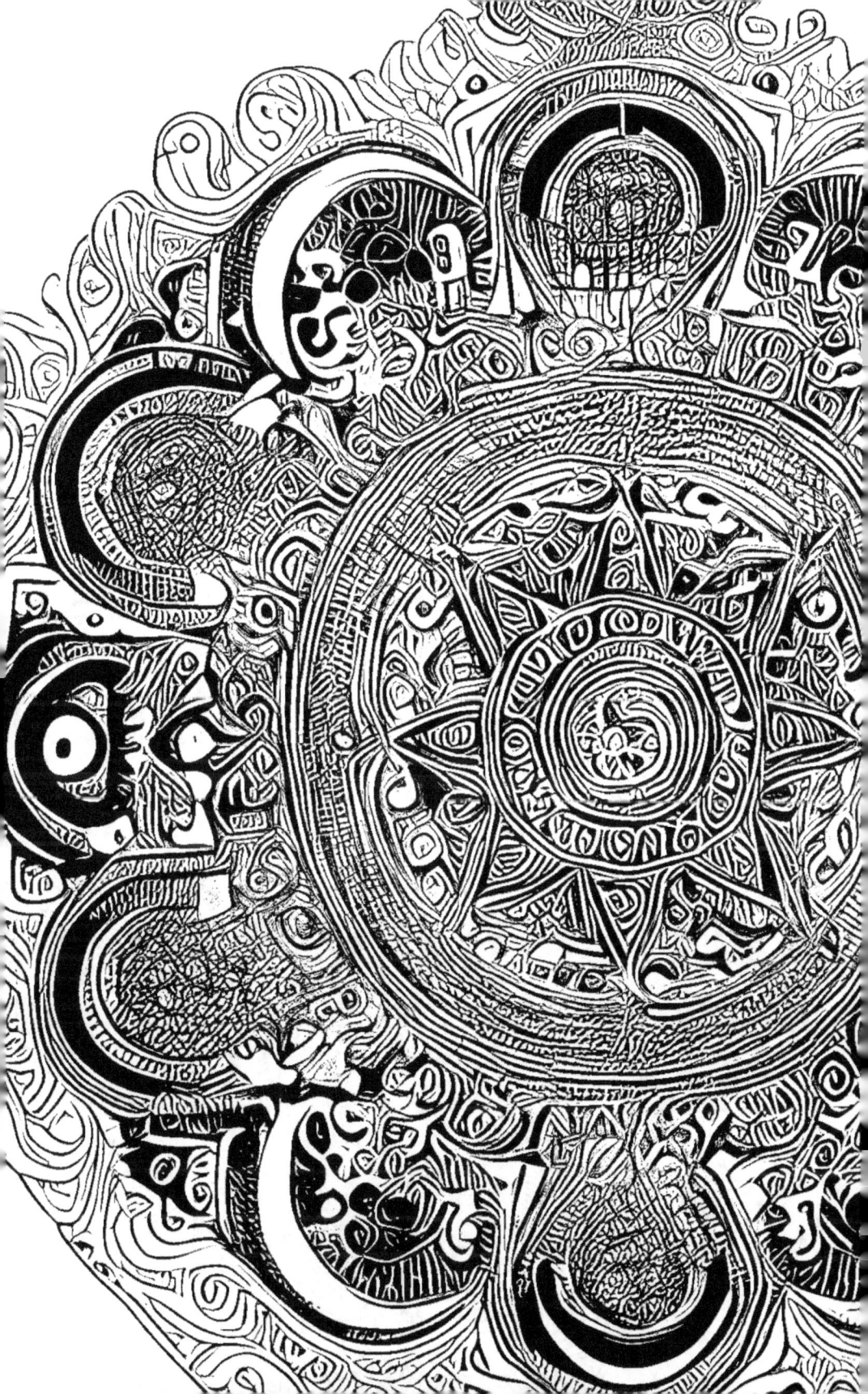

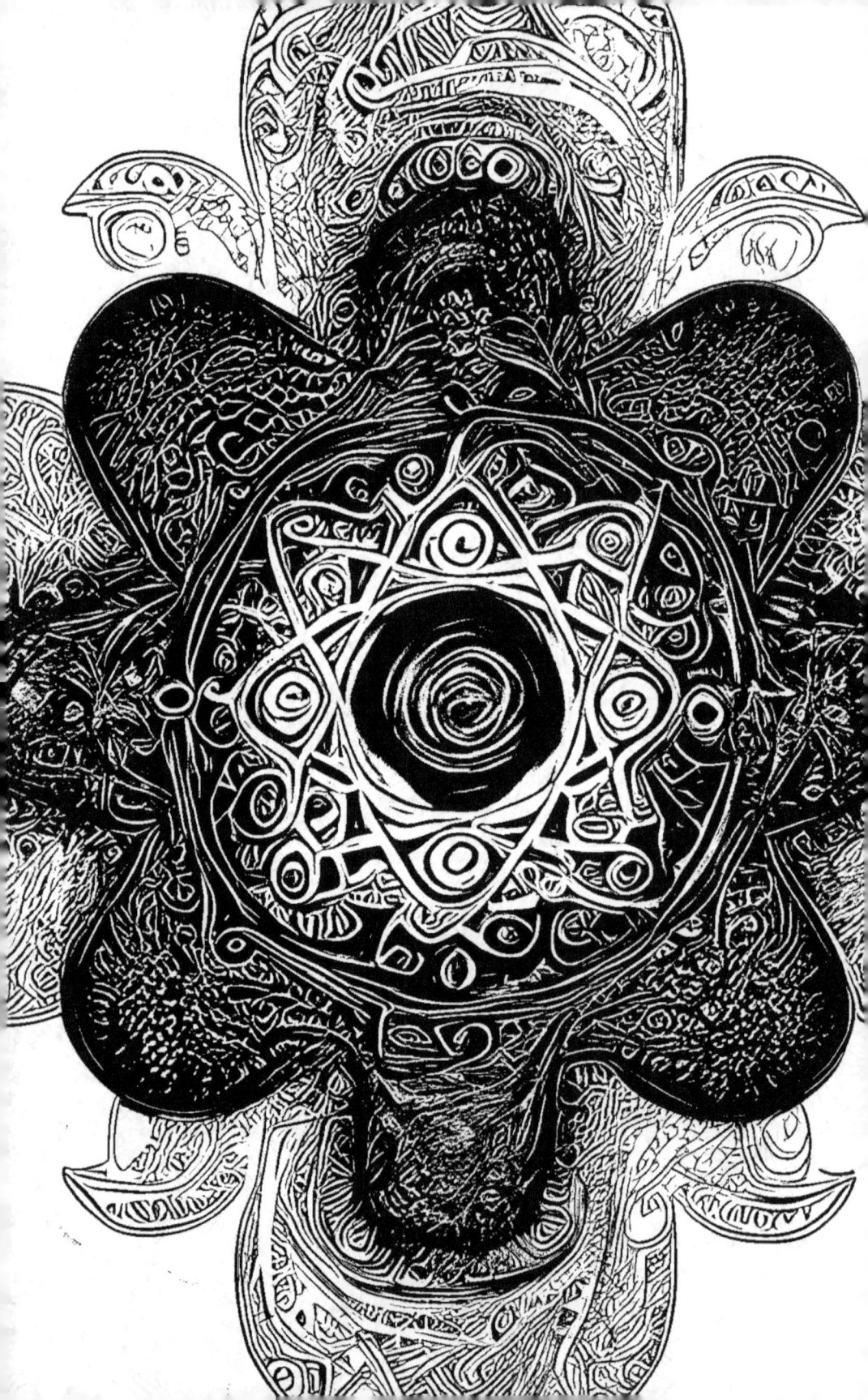

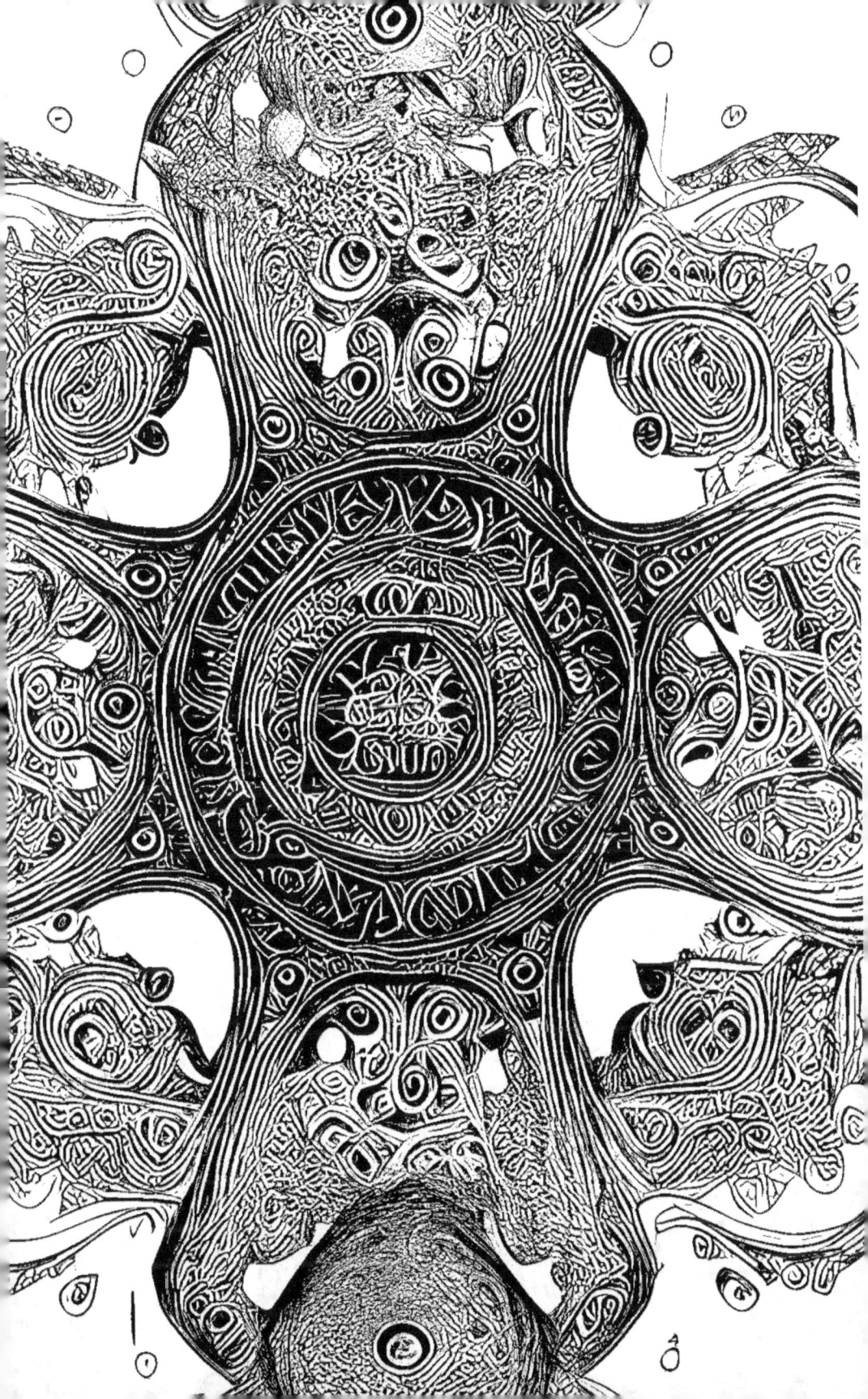

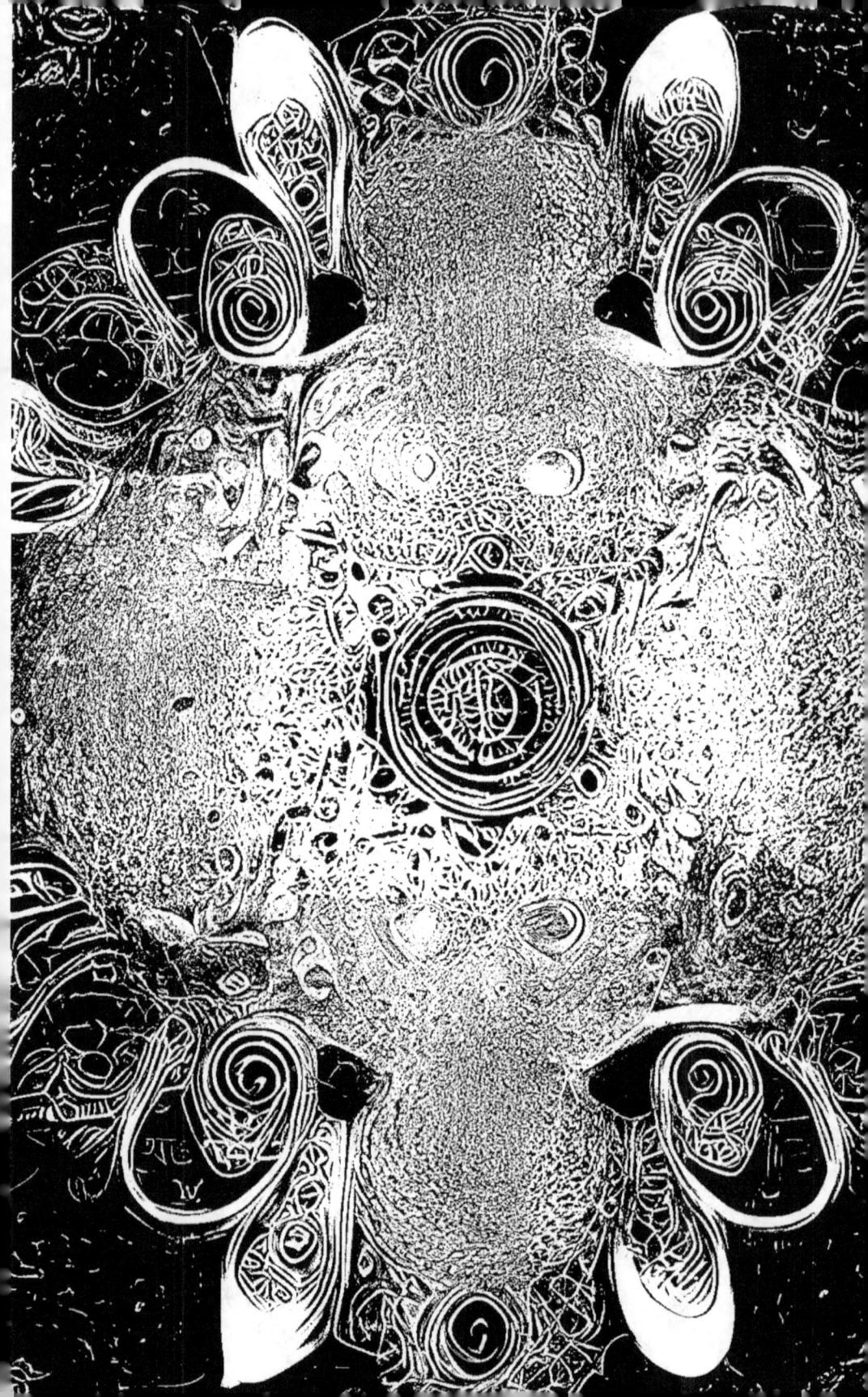

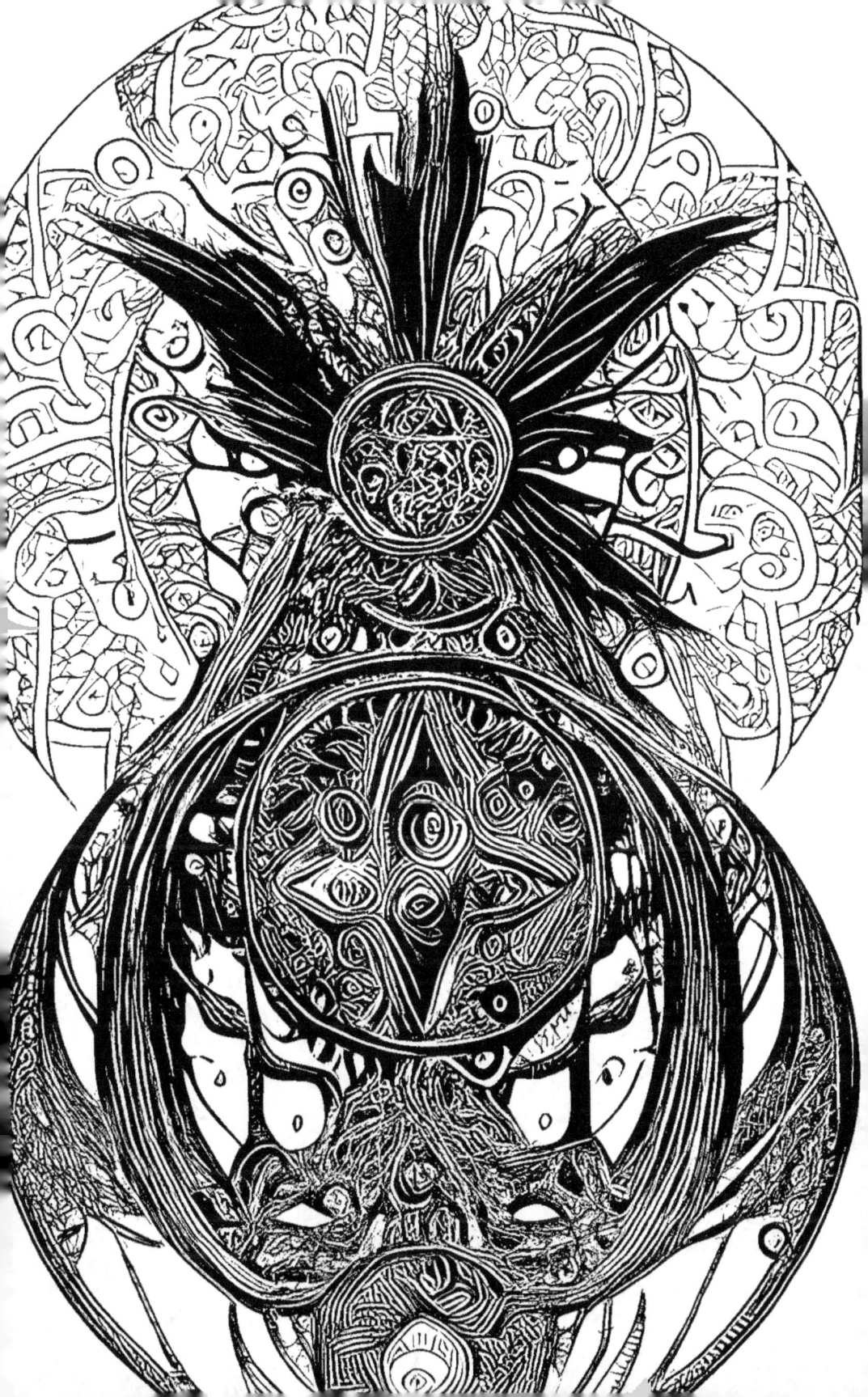

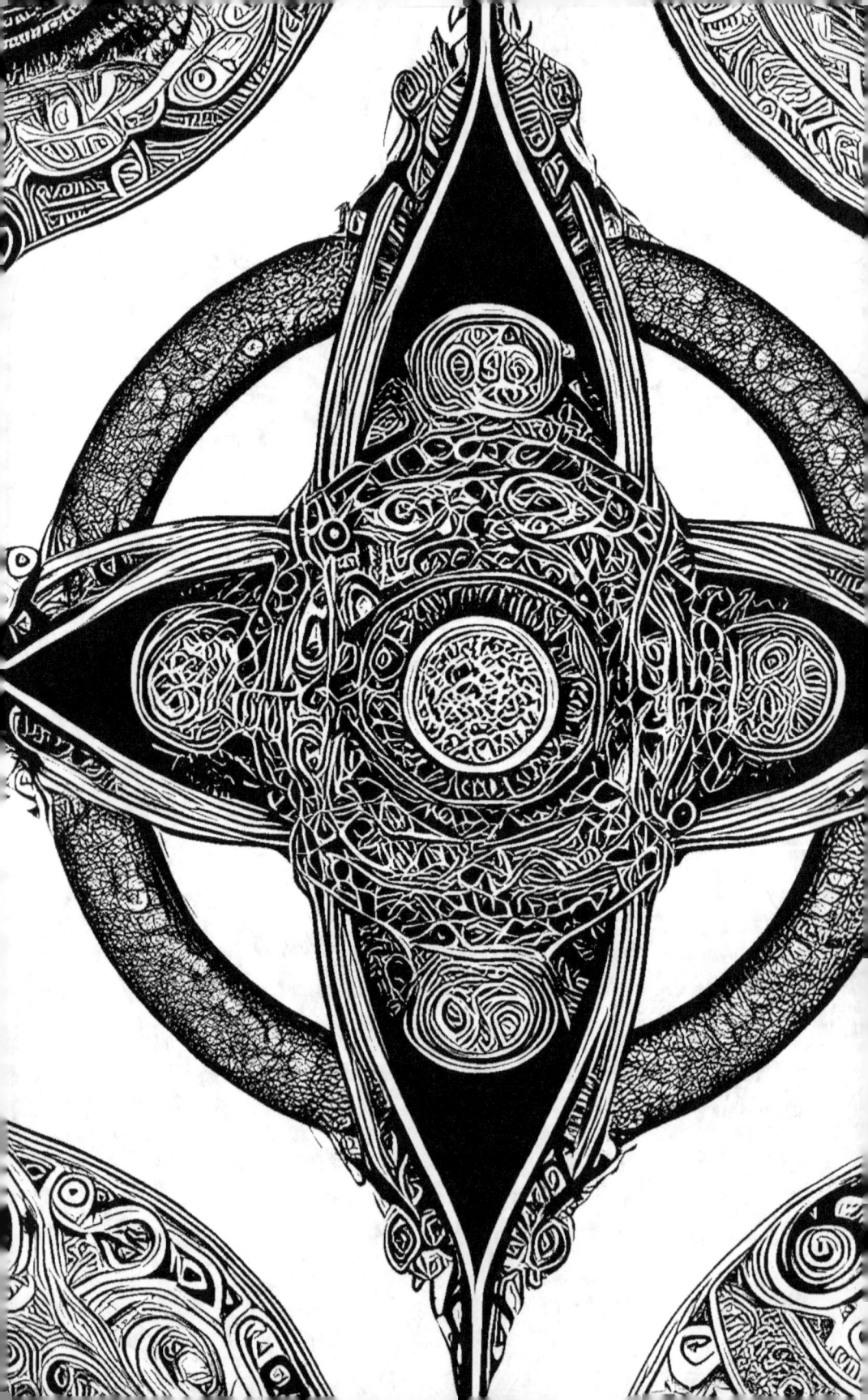

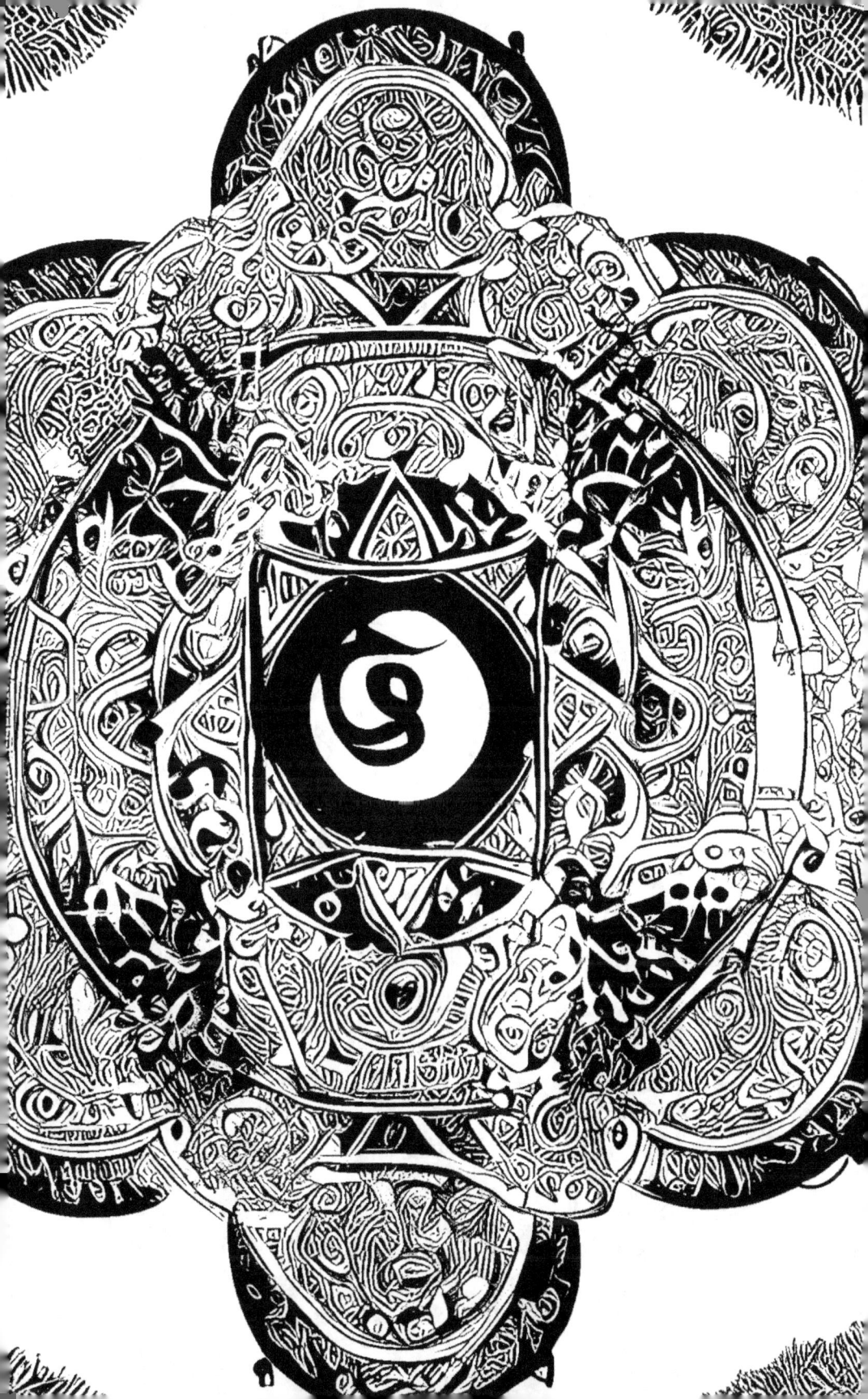

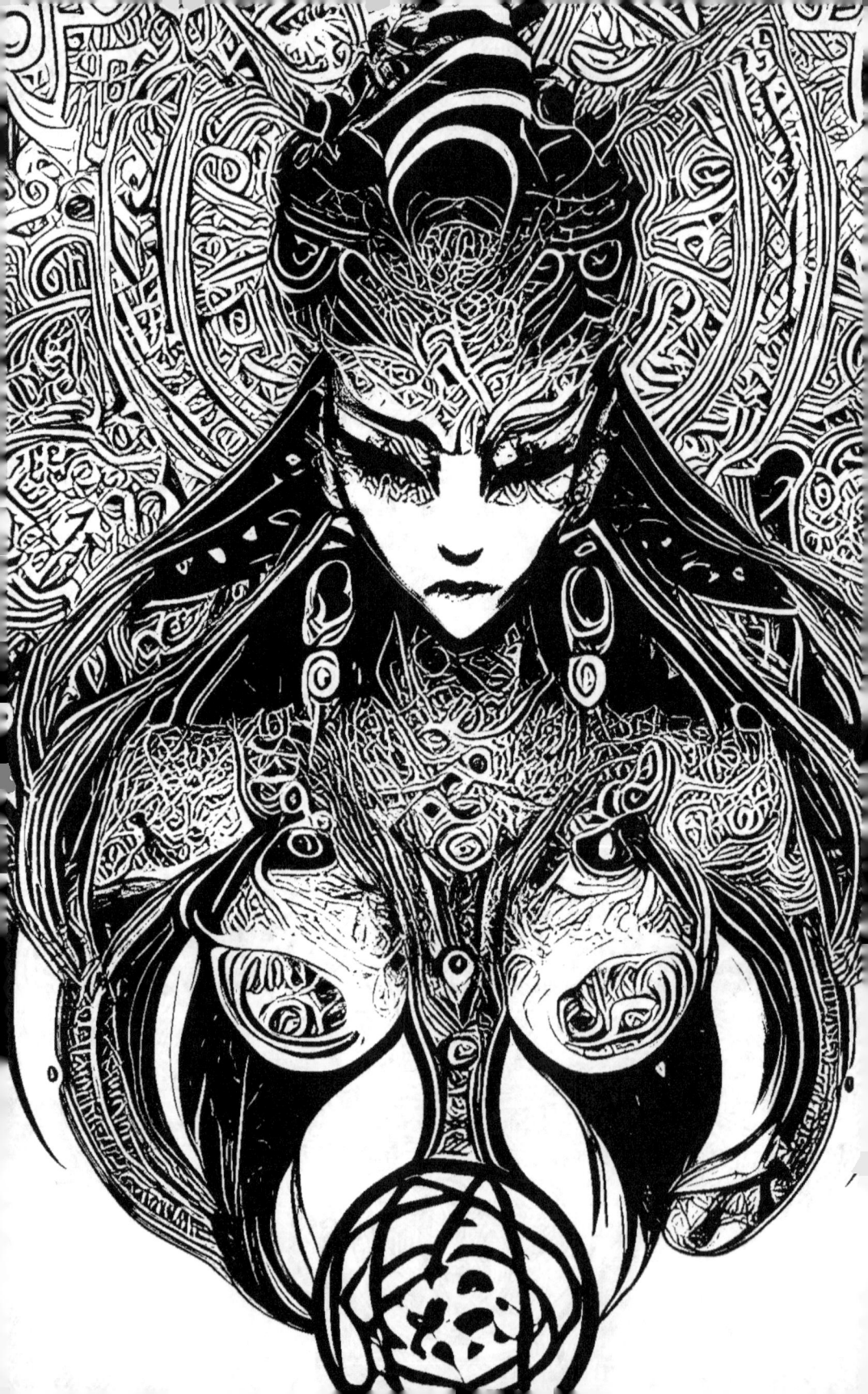

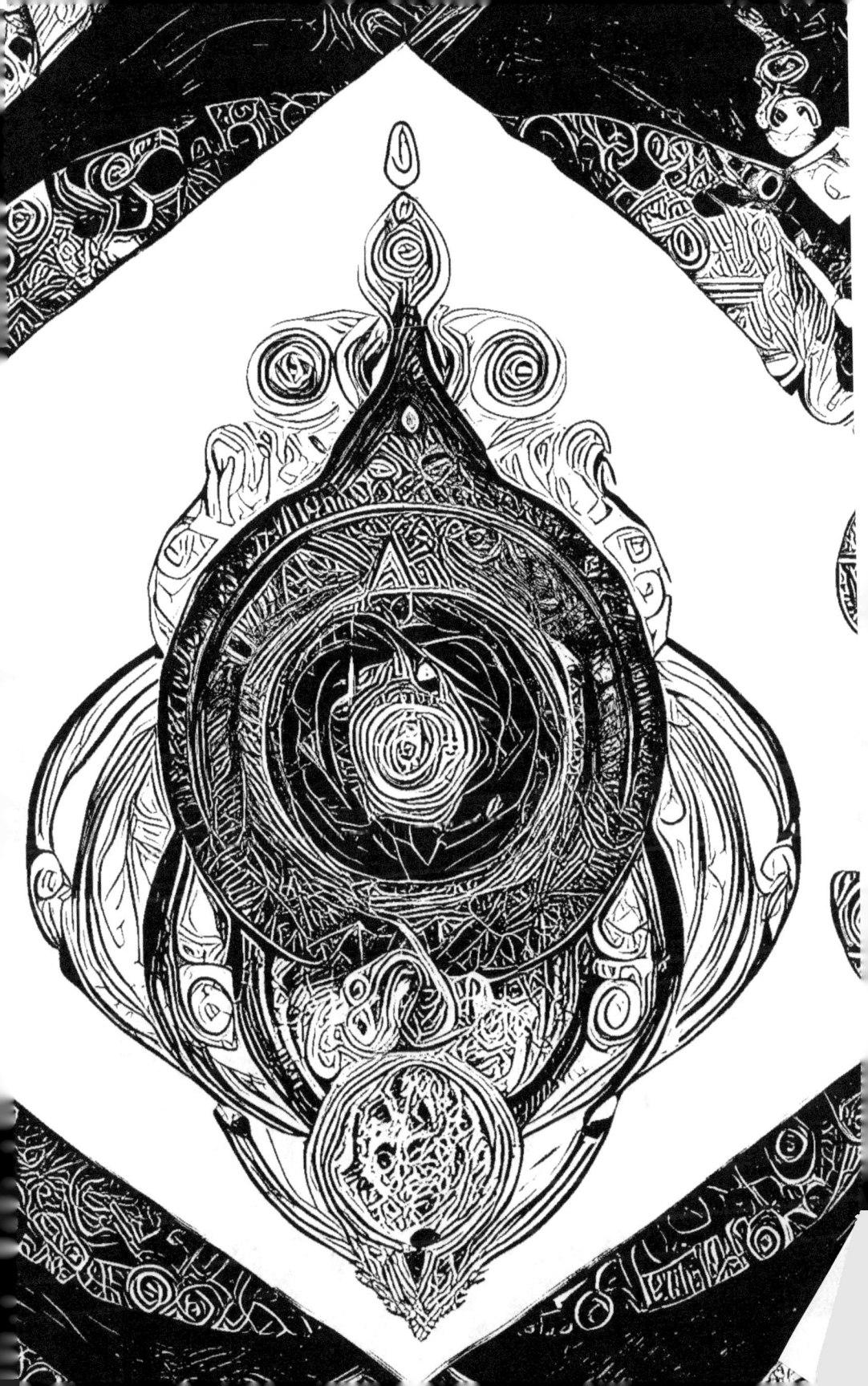

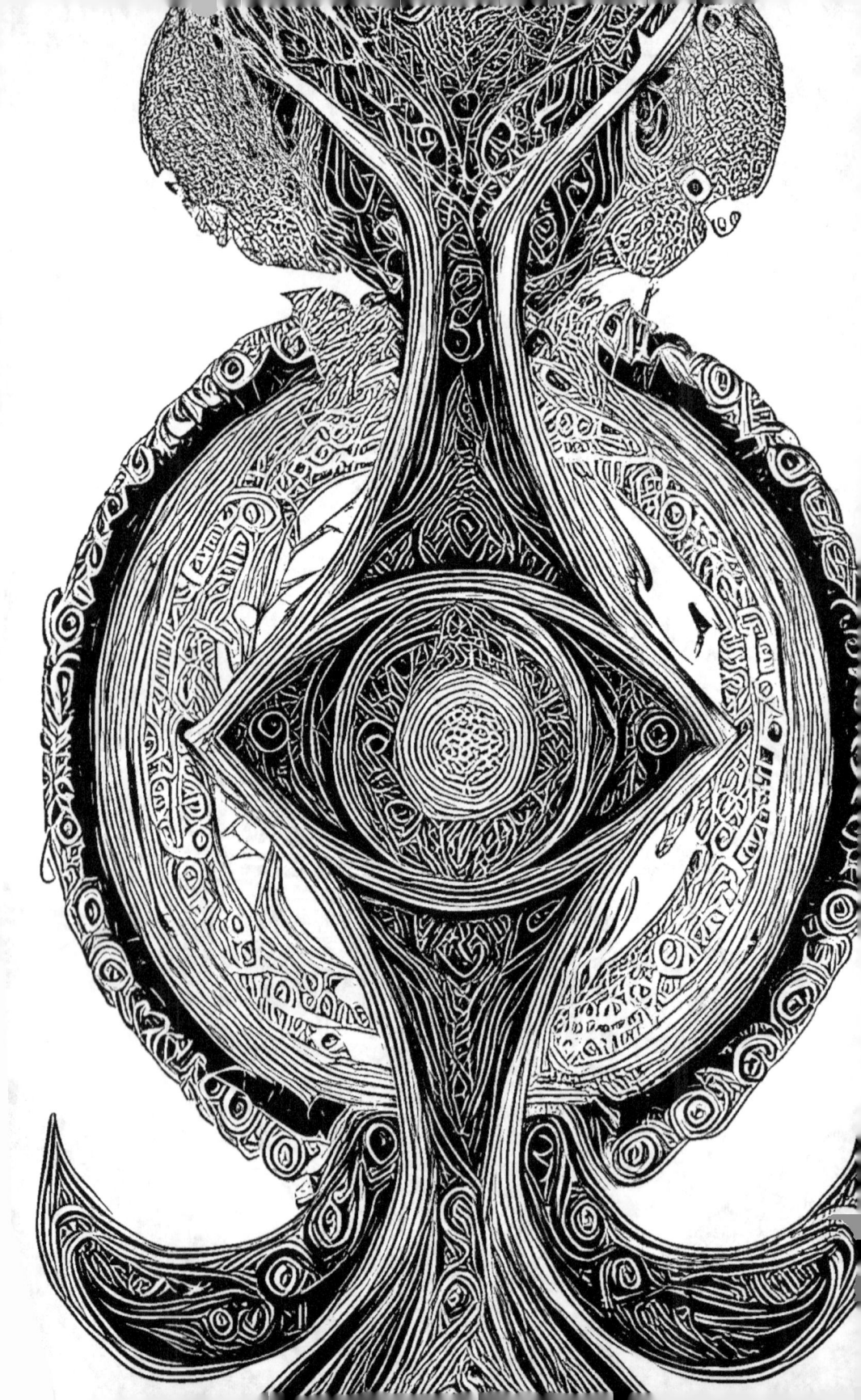

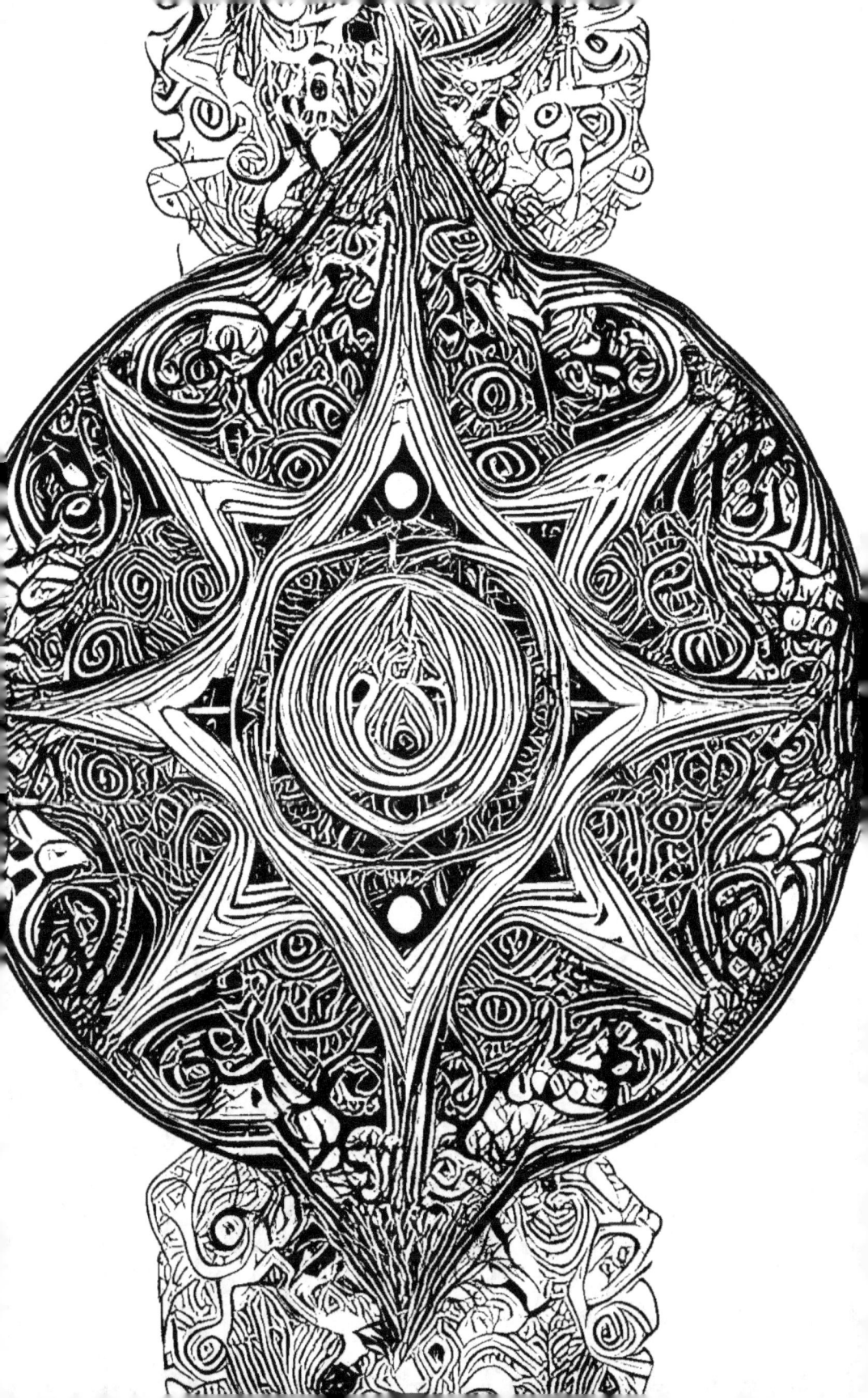

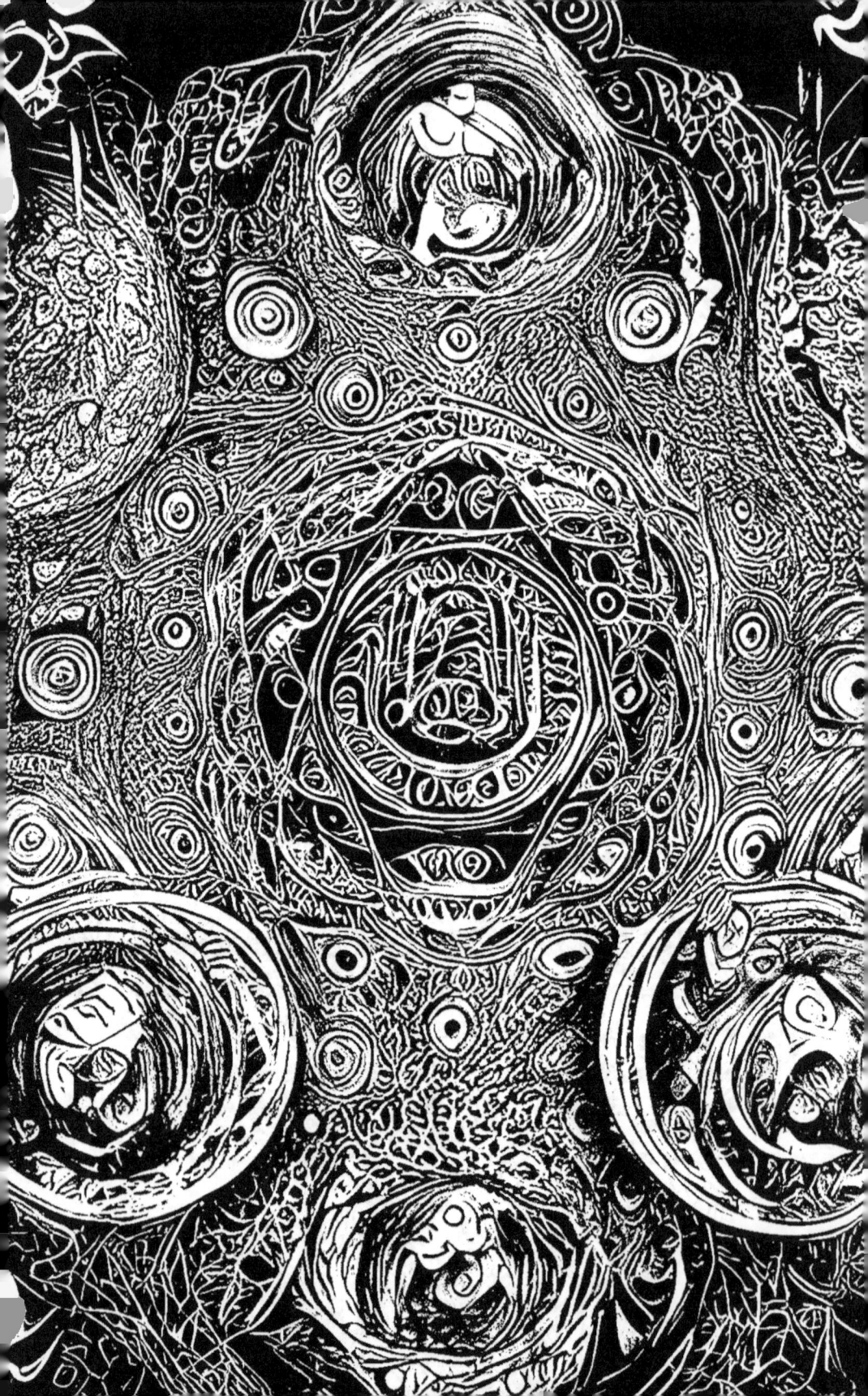

jeremyburt@ishopdailyonline.com jburt_01@hotmail.com
Make Money Online: https://ishopdailyonline.com
Print On Demand: https://ishopdaily.redbubble.com
Print On Demand @ Etsy: https://ishopdailyonline.etsy.com
dj12mind Instrumental Music Albums: https://dj12mind.com
Affiliate Products: https://index.ishopdailyonline.com
Patreon: https://www.patreon.com/user?u=80194438
Facebook: https://www.facebook.com/jeremy.burt2
Youtube:
https://www.youtube.com/channel/UCwV3nApPDh3dNHUGIX4w5nA
tiktok: https://www.tiktok.com/@jeremyburt4?lang=en
amazon: https://www.amazon.com/author/jeremyburt
THANK YOU FOR CHECKING IT OUT!

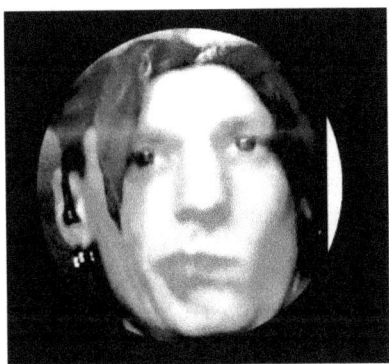

www.ingramcontent.com/pod-product-compliance
Lightning Source LLC
Chambersburg PA
CBHW070907220526
45466CB00005B/2157